SUASIVE ITERATIONS

RHETORIC, WRITING, AND PHYSICAL COMPUTING

David M. Rieder

Parlor Press
Anderson, South Carolina
www.parlorpress.com

Parlor Press LLC, Anderson, South Carolina, USA
© 2017 by Parlor Press
All rights reserved.
Printed in the United States of America on acid-free paper.

SAN: 254-8879

Cataloging-in-Publication Data on File

978-1-60235-568-2 (paperback)
978-1-60235-569-9 (hardcover)
978-1-60235-570-5 (PDF)
978-1-60235-571-2 (ePub)
978-1-60235-572-9 (iBook)
978-1-60235-573-6 (Kindle)

1 2 3 4 5

New Media Theory
Series Editor: Byron Hawk

Cover image: "WiFi Objects" by Nickolay Lamm for MyDeals.com. Used
   by permission.
Book Design: David Blakesley

Parlor Press, LLC is an independent publisher of scholarly and trade titles in print
and multimedia formats. This book is available in paper, cloth and eBook formats from Parlor Press on the World Wide Web at http://www.parlorpress.com or
through online and brick-and-mortar bookstores. For submission information or
to find out about Parlor Press publications, write to Parlor Press, 3015 Bracken-
berry Drive, Anderson, South Carolina, 29621, or email editor@parlorpress.com.

FOR MY FATHER,

DR. RONALD F. RIEDER

Contents

Acknowledgments   *ix*

1 For/Get the Digital (and Ditch the Umbrella)   *3*

2 Transduction and Allegorized Style   *31*

2.5 Writing with Three-Dimensional Wa(y)ves   *59*

3 Onto-Allegories for the 'Great Outdoors'   *66*

3.5 Onto-Allegorized Tweets and the Third (Wayve) State   *92*

4 Plumbing the Paradoxical Depths   *101*

4.5 The Paradoxical Depths of Delivery   *120*

5 A Call for Distant (Transductive) Writing   *127*

5.5 Choric Capacitances   *151*

6 After the Bookish Era of the PC   *159*

Works Cited   *163*
Index   *169*
About the Author   *177*

Acknowledgments

There are many friends, family, and colleagues whom I need to thank for lending me their time, encouragement, and expertise. During the early drafting stages, members of the closed Facebook group, Savants on Sabbatical, helped me stay focused and motivated as I worked out the basic outline and content of my arguments. Susan Miller-Cochran in particular was an immense source of support through those stages of my writing process. Another colleague whom I cannot thank enough is Helen Burgess, who was my copyeditor and mentor in the final stages of the book's development. A few more friends and colleagues who helped me at various stages include Jim Brown, Casey Boyle, Doug Eyman, Sarah Arroyo, Byron Hawk, Dave Blakeseley, Kevin Brock, and Wendi Sierra. I would also like to thank the CRDM PhD students in the spring 2015 seminar, Rhetoric and Digital Media, who read drafts of two chapters and let me demonstrate one of the projects that made it into the book. My biggest thanks are reserved for Shelley Garrigan, who sacrificed her own research time for my success, and my parents, Danièle and Ronald Rieder.

SUASIVE ITERATIONS

1 For/Get the Digital (and Ditch the Umbrella)

It's time to bridge the gap between the physical and the virtual—time to use more than just your fingers to interact with your computer. Step outside of the confines of the basic computer and into the broader world of computing.

—Dan O'Sullivan and Tom Igoe, Physical Computing

It's a hot afternoon in July in New York City, 2013. You have been waiting in line for over five hours to experience an immersive art installation at The Museum of Modern Art (MOMA) titled "Rain Room" (Belcove). Since its opening two months earlier, over 50,000 people have waited in line before you—some for several more hours—to experience one of the most Instagrammed art installations that year (Rabinovitch). Its popularity is one of the reasons that you bought a ticket. The "dramatic, Hollywood-like" pictures and videos from this installation as well as from the inaugural one in 2012 at the Barbican Gallery, London, England, have contributed to your fear of missing out, a.k.a. FOMO (Rabinovitch).

Figure 1. "Rain Room," by Random International. Barbican Gallery, 2012. Video credit: Troshy.

But another reason for waiting in line is a YouTube video of *The Guardian*'s Architecture and Design critic Oliver Wainwright's walkthrough in 2012, in which he offered the following remarks:

3

It's really surreal. Not only is it raining indoors, but I'm not even getting the slightest bit wet wherever I go. It's almost like I'm giving off some kind of wind that's pushing the rain away, like I'm a human whirlwind. ["Rain Room"] somehow responds to me like I have a magnetic field. Wherever I go, it opens up around me. ("Barbican's Rain Room")

You want to experience something as novel as walking through a downpour without getting wet, which reminds you of descriptions of miraculous acts of water walking in several religious and fictional texts.

When you finally enter the dark, damp installation space, you and nine other participants have a ten-minute window of opportunity to engage with it. You notice that a larger group of participants are cordoned off behind a rope; the line to enter was shorter for them, but they can only watch. The installation is over 300 feet in length with a bright spotlight at the far end. The floor beneath you is a grate into which the rain falls. Looking up from where you are standing, you see that the simulated rain storm is based on a drop ceiling made up of hundreds of water valves. A few people in the space have gathered together to speculate about the technical design of the installation. Another two are taking selfies. Two more, who were holding hands, have started slow dancing together.

As you stand alone in the middle of the space, meditating on the experience of "Rain Room," you realize that you are participating in a new form of popular computing, one in which invention or creativity is based on the ability to identify the available means of blurring the conventional line between the physical and virtual worlds. "Rain Room" may be a dramatic example of this new approach to what is called physical computing, but we are increasingly engaged and immersed in these kinds of hybrid realities, thanks to the growing number of smart, sensory-based, wireless, networked technologies in our everyday lives.

Suasive Iterations offers digital rhetors and writers, digital media artists, and "digital humanists 2.0" a method of rhetorical invention and creativity within this new paradigm of popular computing. Physical computing is a relatively new computational paradigm in which practitioners build interactive objects and environments that can both sense and respond to the analog world. It is a computational approach predicated on blurring the conventional line between the virtual or digital realm and the "real," physical or analog world. There are a number of other terms associated with this computational approach including ubiquitous computing (ubicomp), pervasive computing, ambient computing, Internet of Things (IoT), wearable computing, "everyware," and natural-user interface (NUI) design. In

For/Get the Digital (and Ditch the Umbrella)

this book, I offer an approach that all of the abovementioned terms share, which is to transform the conventional ways we experience and engage with the real by finding new ways to fold some of the affordances of the virtual into it. Whether "wearable," NUI, or ubicomp "smartifact," these and other technological approaches to the physical hybridize the conventional space-times in which we are engaged. There is no longer a conventional, binary relationship between the analog and digital, and this realization put into practice transforms our sense of self and those relations comprising our interactions with objects and environments.

While the argument that we are now living in hybrid realities is not new, it has become more relevant with the growing popularity of physical computing technologies. William Gibson's use of the term "eversion" in the recent past, for example, demonstrates that he has recognized the shift to a more nuanced experience and engagement with the virtual. In 1982, in his short story "Burning Chrome," Gibson coined the term "cyberspace" to describe a virtual realm separate and distinct from the real (195). Since then, he has adopted the term "eversion" to describe the process of hybridization that now characterizes the relationship between cyberspace and the physical realm:

> Cyberspace, not so long ago, was a specific elsewhere, one we visited periodically, peering into it from the familiar physical world. Now cyberspace has everted. Turned itself inside out. Colonized the physical. ("Google's Earth")

Citing Gibson's quote above, Steven E. Jones underscores the cultural shift in perception of which eversion is expressive. Jones writes,

> [eversion] articulates a widely experienced shift in our collective understanding of the network during the last decade: inside out, from a world apart to a part of the world, from a transcendent virtual reality to mundane experience, from a mysterious, invisible abstract world to a still mostly invisible (but real) data-grid that we move through everyday in the physical world. (19)

The shift to an era of physical computing is one in which innovation is defined by the ability to evert reality, and to creatively bend the conventional experience of reality toward some suasive end, by folding into it some of the affordances of the virtual. Such innovation can be fairly mundane, subtly enhancing an aspect of our everyday practices, or it can lead to a more dramatic shift in how we experience our sense of self and world, as occurs in "Rain Room."

A theme that emerges at several points in this book is the need to innovate beyond the personal computing (PC) era. The PC era "normed" us to the computer anchored to our desk, lap, or hands: the all-in-one personal machine through which we did everything. It inaugurated an era of centripetal computing by establishing the distinction between the virtual and the real, and turning us inwardly toward the former. The cliché of the PC user surfing vast spaces in a virtual world while slumped over a keyboard and mouse is indicative of the extent to which the era interpellated its users to a computational world distinct and disconnected from the everyday. The notion that a commitment to the virtual necessitates a disavowal of the "real" is symptomatic of that era.

The title of this chapter is an implicit call to move beyond (forget) the exclusive focus on the digital that is reinforced by the constraints of the PC era, in order to engage (get) with the new, "everted" realities before us. The new era virtualizes our everyday experiences and expectations, but it does not ask us to disavow the world around us; rather, it integrates the virtual into it. In contrast to the PC era, the new era is centrifugal.

Two popular examples of the new era include FitBit's fitness bracelets and the Waze app. In both cases, the technologies blur the stark distinction between the virtual and real. FitBit's activity bracelet tracks and records its user's daily movements and activities without any direct interaction. There is no keyboard, mouse, or speaker. The microcomputer is meant to work with the user's "lifestyle." Similarly, the Waze app crowdsources real-time traffic patterns from its users by uploading locative data from a phone to Waze's network without direct input. In Figure 2 below, the red-colored street labeled "13 mph" is generated from the speed at which users' GPS-based movements are changing. The data is sent by the app without user input. The avatars are fellow "Wazers" who are currently on the road nearby.

Both of these technologies point to another reason for making the shift to a post-PC era of computational innovation, which is that PC-based computing (the PC era), has peaked. The majority of new, cutting-edge research in digital media is shifting away from the all-in-one computer. We are shifting to a paradigm in which inexpensive sensors, actuators, and microcontrollers (microtechnologies that can sense and act on the analog world) collapse the boundaries established during the PC era between the real and the virtual. Based on these technologies, innovation is now defined by novel ways that we transform our lived reality. Eversion is a sign of success.

For/Get the Digital (and Ditch the Umbrella)

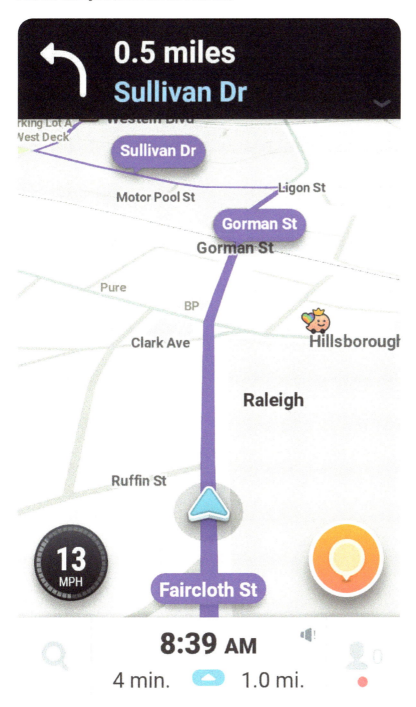

Figure 2. Screen capture of real-time traffic in Waze. *Waze – GPS, Maps & Social Traffic.* Waze Inc., 2015.

The signs of the imminent paradigm shift are nowhere more obvious than in the popularity of tablets and smartphones. Unbeknownst to many users, they are a border technology between the old and new ways of computing. Like PCs, tablets and smartphones are designed to elicit a personal investment from their owners. They contribute to what Nick Montfort calls "screen essentialism" ("Continuous Paper"), which contributes to the narcissistic, gadget-loving gaze that is characteristic of the era. This centripetal gaze, however, blinds us to the dozen or more sensors and cloud-based processes with which those "personal" devices constantly communicate at the periphery of our attention. Our phones and tablets are repeatedly checking our email and social media accounts for updates, transmitting our geolocations to companies and services to which we're subscribed, and monitoring ambient changes in or around the hardware itself. While we devote our attention to the data represented on the screens of our phones and tablets, our phones are busily sensing, transmitting, and receiving a far wider range of data to and from the global cloud.

For most contemporary rhetors and writers, the PC era is the only one in which we've worked. A review of the journal *Computers and Composition* shows that that many of its issues have been about personal computing and composition. During the first six years of the journal (1983-1989), word processing software on IBM-compatible and Apple PCs was a persistent topic. In the early 1990s, the focus began to shift to hypertextual and hypermedia software, and those new forms of writing were practiced on PCs. MOOing, too, became an important topic, and while the MOO foregrounded multi-user networked computing, the desktop computer was the interface through which it was accessed. In the mid-1990s, Cynthia Selfe and Richard Selfe's article "The Politics of the Interface" focused on the politics of the desktop computing interface, thus reinforcing the power of desktop computing as the epitome of the PC era (64).

By the early 2000s, topics associated with internet-based communication shared journal space with web-based approaches to composition, augmented by a growing range of socio-cultural, political, and pedagogical approaches to digital media—including games. Nonetheless, the personal computer was the generic platform for engagement. As multimodality and new media studies showed up alongside the ever-growing range of topics in the mid- to late-2000s, the PC remained a persistent platform for theory and practice in our field. And by the mid-2010s, when the focus of the journal now includes handheld computing devices such as tablets and smartphones, the approach is still principally PC-based.

For/Get the Digital (and Ditch the Umbrella)

Four Technologies of the Post-PC Era

From a technological standpoint, there are four technologies that are essential for innovation in the post-PC era. The first are input technologies: microtechnological components known as sensors, which are designed to sense specific kinds of physical energy. There are sensors for ambient energy changes (temperature, humidity, light, movement, and more) as well as for direct user interaction.

The passive infrared (PIR) motion sensor is an example of the former. It is a ubiquitous technology in home security systems, classrooms, hallways, and public bathrooms. The sensor detects changes to the infrared radiation pattern in a space, which is the basis for defining changes in motion. The sensor is used conventionally to turn on floodlights outside a home, or to turn on or off the lights in a public space.

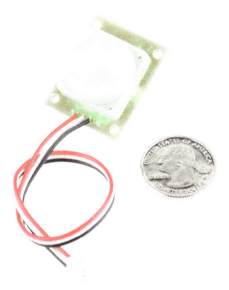

Figure 3. Passive infrared (PIR) motion sensor. Photo credit: SparkFun Electronics.

Input technologies that facilitate direct user interaction include the keys on a keyboard, rotary and slide potentiometers (see Figure 4 below), the touchscreen on a smartphone, and all of the various kinds of buttons, switches, dials, cameras, and microphones with which we interact everyday. When we interact with one of the sensors, the energy flows associated with them are changed.

Figure 4. A slide potentiometer (pot).

Understanding generally how sensors work will allow us to understand an important technical basis for eversion. Sensors are microcomponents within an electrical circuit, which means that they have a specific and continuous amount of electricity passing across them at all times. Sensors are designed to produce changes to the continuous flow of electrical voltage across their surface. Thus if I have written a software program that is monitoring the number of volts running across a circuit in which the sensor is placed, any changes to that continuous, analog voltage will represent a change in the "real" world the sensor is designed to detect. The two energy flows—the one in the "real" world affecting the sensor and the electrical current flowing across it—are related.

The second kind of technologies are output devices, or actuators, which are microcomponents and mechanisms that can act in the "real" world. In other words, they can make sound, create light, and, with DC motors, move objects. Actuators include everything from small LED status lights to large screens and projectors, buzzers, speakers, and motors.

For/Get the Digital (and Ditch the Umbrella)

Figure 5. Basic yellow 3mm LED. Photo credit: SparkFun Electronics.

The third technology is methodological: the process of transduction. That process can occur in hardware or software. In this book, it is software-based. Dan O'Sullivan and Tom Igoe explain that transduction is "about creating a conversation between the physical world and the virtual world of the computer" (xix). In their book, *Physical Computing: Sensing and Controlling the Physical World with Computers*, they elaborate on the meaning of their term and the goal with which it is associated:

> The process of transduction, or the conversion of one form of energy into another, is what enables this flow. Your job is to find, and learn to use, transducers to convert between physical energy appropriate for your project and the electrical energy used by the computer. (xix-xx)

In a physical computing project, the software programs that a rhetor writes are the basis for transductions of energy to and from the analog and the digital. Those software programs transduce the flow of energy in order to create a conversation between the physical and virtual. When William Gibson writes about the eversion of cyberspace, and about the colonization of the physical, he is implicitly writing about the impact of transductive processes. When the virtual and the real are folded together in some novel way, a moment of transduction has occurred. Eversion is the expression of a transductive process.

These three technologies—sensors (inputs), actuators (outputs), and transductive processes—are the basis for numerous physical computing projects, including the abovementioned "Rain Room." In order to understand the technological bases of "Rain Room," we can turn to the above-cited critic Oliver Wainwright. After his walkthrough, Wainwright asks the two artists who designed the project, Florian Ortkrass and Jeremy Wood, how it works. "How do I not get wet walking straight through the middle?" he asks. Wood explains, "The piece is tracked using 3D depth cameras. Essentially, as you walk in, you become a shape and a body. And then it turns individual valves on and off that we have above the piece" ("Barbican's Rain Room"). Wood is describing the transductive process that is the basis for Wainwright's "surreal," everted experience. Analog data from a group of sensors (3D depth cameras) are transduced by software, which then controls the flow of water from the actuators (individual valves) above the space. A transductive conversation has been successfully developed in which the real and the virtual are folded together.

If we look at the physical reality that "Rain Room" everts—if, in other words, we focus on the suasive aspects of the project—the digital project reconstitutes the perceived gap between a body and its surrounding world that is otherwise unavailable to us in a rainstorm. When we are caught in a rainstorm, the gap between self and world collapses and the "hereness" of our bodies is inescapable and conspicuous. We lose our sense of perspective, our mindfulness. "Rain Room" reinstates the gap or distance that is a necessary to examine and reflect on an experience. The joy and wonder that participants describe after walking through "Rain Room" suggest that they have regained a sense of mindfulness and perspective conventionally lost in a rainstorm. The transductive process introduces some of the affordances of the virtual—the same kinds of affordances that let avatars defy gravity in a computer game or types of actions that defy the conventions of space and time. The recreated gap is a transduced eversion.

The fourth technology of the post-PC era is wireless, internet-based communications. With "Rain Room," the transductive process appears to be confined to the local. The "conversation" in which the sensors, software, and actuators are engaged does not appear to extend beyond the gallery space. But when the first three aspects of a physical computing project are designed to communicate distally with "the cloud," the sensors and actuators associated with one or more physical objects comprise an object that is global in character.

A sample physical computing project that uses wireless communication to participate in a global process of transduction is the Good Night Lamp.

For/Get the Digital (and Ditch the Umbrella)

Figure 6. The Good Night Lamp™ (2015). Photo credit: Good Night Lamp™.

This project is a wireless network of lamps, consisting of a "big" lamp and one or more "little" lamps. The big and little lamps participate in a single, cloud-based network. All of the lamps in the network have an actuator built into them (a light), as well as Wi-Fi capability. At the top of the chimney on the big lamp is a pushbutton sensor. When the sensor on the big lamp is pressed, the actuator in each of the little lamps will turn on or off, depending on its current state. In a video promoting the lamps, founder Alexandra Deschamps-Sonsino describes several uses for the lamps, including the following two: "You can give a big lamp to your daughter, so you can see whenever she goes to sleep at night. You can also give one to your partner, so when they leave work, you know that you can start dinner or you can give them a call to arrange what to do that evening" (Good Night Lamp).

From the perspective of the transductive process, when the pushbutton is pressed, the sensor transduces the physical action of pressing the button into a change in voltage in that part of the circuit. The voltage is soon after transduced into a digital value. Several more transduction's later, the digital value representative of the voltage change is sent to a cloud-based software program running distally, which, in turn, transduces it again, communicating the state change to all of the little lamps. When the Wi-Fi capable computer in each of the little lamps receives a new command from the cloud, it transduces that command into a change in the voltage in that part of the circuit, and the light turns on or off.

Whereas the eversion generated by the transductive technologies in "Rain Room" recreates the lived distance between a body and its surroundings, the Good Night Lamp collapses the physical distance between two or more friends, colleagues, or family members. When a little house lights up, it signals to the viewer that a physical action or energy attributed to a specific person in another place (and time zone) has been transduced and communicated across the cloud. That sense of proximity is the expression of an eversion of the conventional distance between users.

For Aristotle, rhetoric is the discovery of the available means of persuasion. For digital rhetors, discovering the available means of transduction is the basis for invention. Eversion is the outcome as well as the moment of suasion. The ability to transduce physical energy from the physical world (sensors), transduce it again locally or remotely (the cloud) in one or more software programs, and then transduce it back into the physical world (actuators) is how a rhetor folds the virtual into the real, thereby generating an everted experience.

Transductive Rhetoric and Writing: Stretching the Truth

For scholars in rhetoric and composition—even those of us affiliated with the field of computers and writing—the new era of physical computing is a challenging one to reconcile with our scholarly and pedagogical training. Many of us relate to the virtual realm of the computer through our PCs—and while that realm is highly social and networked, it is not explicitly engaged with the wide range of transductive sensors and actuators that make projects like Rain Room possible. We are not used to working toward the rhetorical goal of everting an audience's experience through a technical process of designing circuits and writing code to transduce or convert physical energy.

In addition to the above-mentioned challenges, digital rhetors and writers may find it difficult to reconcile our language-based theories and practices with the new computational era. This is because the new era of physical computing includes many technologies and computational approaches that are not based in linguistic or textual forms of knowing and communication. It is especially due to this constraint that rhetors and writers who want to establish an explicit connection between physical computing and the field of rhetoric and composition must "casuistically stretch" some of its definitions and practices. Casuistry, Kenneth Burke once argued, is "the application of abstract principles to particular conditions" (155). The inherent challenge facing any act of casuistry is that generic principles do

For/Get the Digital (and Ditch the Umbrella)

not always fit the specific circumstances in which they will be applied. James Jasinski explains the challenge as follows:

> Principles are not applied to cases in a mechanistic manner . . . contemporary theorists speak frequently of the idea of adjusting principles to cases or negotiating the relationship between principle and case. (89)

For Burke, casuistic stretching is a process in which "one introduces new principles while theoretically remaining faithful to old principles" (230). If a well-established theory of rhetoric and persuasion can be stretched to fit the "specific circumstances" of the new era of physical computing, eversion becomes established as an explicitly suasive act, and the transductive process framed as a new approach to invention within the creative framework of physical computing.

There are three scholarly sources that stand out as strong candidates for casuistic stretching because they would help reconcile rhetorical theory and practice with the new era of computing. The first is Lloyd Bitzer's well-known essay, "The Rhetorical Situation." In that essay, Bitzer explains that rhetoric "functions ultimately to produce action or change in the world," and that it is a "mode of altering reality" (3-4). If we stopped with these two quotes, extending a Bitzerian principle of rhetoric to eversion would not require any stretching. Transduction is the process by which action or change is produced, and a reality-altering, everted experience is its outcome. But in the same sentence in which he defines rhetoric as a mode of altering reality, Bitzer explicitly states that it is "not by the direct application of energy to objects, but by the creation of discourse" (4). Why explicitly deny an association with energy? I would hazard a guess that Bitzer did not want his definition of rhetoric to be confused with disciplines in which the application of energy on objects is central. But limiting rhetoric to the discursive realm is now problematic. First, it inadvertently perpetuates the "two cultures" split between the humanities and the sciences, even while the era of physical computing demands that we bridge that gap in order to innovate. It also does not reflect where innovation tends to occur under the auspices of digital media arts, digital humanities, and digital rhetoric. Fifty years after the publication of his essay, innovation in the arts and humanities has become increasingly associated with techniques and technologies that would traditionally be associated with STEM disciplines. In an era of physical computing, if rhetoric is defined as a mode of altering reality, it should include the transductive process of energy conversions. For these reasons, Bitzer's theory needs to be casuistically stretched.

Suasive Iterations

A second issue with Bitzer's theory is related to his conceptualization of place, which Jenny Edbauer has addressed in her essay, "Unframing Models of Public Distribution: From Rhetorical Situation to Rhetorical Ecologies." While Bitzer's situational theory was a compelling update to the sender-receiver models of communication, Edbauer argues, his implicit notion of place does not adequately account for the nuanced, affective dimensions of communication, social relations, and rhetorics in today's networked society. Situational models of persuasion like Bitzer's conceptualize place as a local and discrete container in which rhetoric happens. Extending a point that she develops from Steven Shaviro's *Connected, or What It Means to Live in the Network Society*, Edbauer explains the inherent embeddedness of social existence:

> [N]etworks involve a different kind of habitation in the social field. To say that we are connected is another way of saying that we are never outside the networked interconnection of forces, energies, rhetorics, moods, and experiences. In other words, our practical consciousness is never outside the prior and ongoing structures of feeling that shape the social field. (10)

Building upon Edbauer's observations, I argue that an era of physical computing is more directly engaged with the "ongoing structures of feeling that shape a social field." The feelings of joy and excitement associated with "Rain Room" are a case in point. The interrelated processes of transduction and eversion contribute to a change in the conventional structure of feelings in the social realm. When a rhetor designs an everted experience from the available means of transduction, she has altered reality and reshaped the social field, which means that she has been persuasive.

Returning to Bitzer's definition of rhetoric as a (discursive) mode of altering reality, Bitzer writes, "The rhetor alters reality by bringing into existence a discourse of such a character that the audience, in thought and action, is so engaged that it becomes mediator of change. In this sense rhetoric is always persuasive" (4). Casuistically stretching that definition so that it fits the new era of computing, a neo-Bitzerian reading of rhetoric could be as follows: when a rhetor transduces the energies conventionally associated with a mode of reality (read: a structure of feeling), the audience experiences a change in reality, thereby contributing to epistemic and discursive changes. In this way, a transductive rhetoric of eversion is always persuasive.

The second candidate for casuistic stretching is Lawrence W. Rosenfield's approach to epideictic, in his essay, "The Practical Celebration of Epideictic." Rosenfield's approach to epideictic helps justify the suasive goals of a physical computing project, but it needs to be stretched beyond its

For/Get the Digital (and Ditch the Umbrella)

oratorical context. Epideictic is known as the third branch of oratory. The two preceding it are the deliberative and forensic. Traditionally, deliberative oratory has been associated with politics, forensic with the law, and epideictic with ceremonial occasions. Additionally, the three branches are associated with the three temporalities: deliberative oratory is concerned with the future, forensic with the past, and epideictic with the present. When a politician expounds on something she will do for her audience, she speaks deliberatively toward the future. When a lawyer for the defense rebuts the facts surrounding a past event, her discourse is forensic. And when a speaker eulogizes the passing of a loved one at at memorial, stands up to offer a few words during a toast at a wedding reception, or roasts a friend at a party to celebrate his promotion at work, her words are epideictic; they are meant for the current moment.

Rosenfield's essay begins as a rebuttal against the devaluations of epideictic in rhetoric theory. He writes, "I believe that epideictic served a more significant theoretical role than as a wastebasket for classifying lesser orations in the rhetorical domain" (133). Rosenfield is referring to the way in which rhetoric scholars had treated the third branch of oratory as superficial and even inferior:

> Many list it dutifully as one of the ancient forms of public address, but then pass on quickly to deliberative and forensic oratory, leaving the impression that epideictic is an afterthought meant to cover those orations that are unable to fit neatly into one of the two major classifications. (131)

Even more troubling than its marginalization is its explicit devaluation as an inconsequential form of rhetoric. Rosenfield offers two examples. The first, which he characterizes as the "conventional wisdom on the topic" (131), is from E.M. Cope's *An Introduction to Aristotle's Rhetoric*. Cope describes epideictic as inferior because it is "demonstrative, showy, ostentatious." Epideictic speeches are "composed for 'show' or 'exhibition'" and "their object is to display the orator's powers, and to amuse an audience . . . who are therefore *theorio* rather than *kritai*, like spectators at a theater" (Cope 121; Rosenfield 131).

About the second example, Rosenfield writes, "Nowhere is epideictic's domain more diminished than in Chaim Perelman's interpretation" (132). In Perelman and L. Olbrechts-Tyteca's *The New Rhetoric*, epideictic is reduced to a form of amusement. Rosenfield quotes the following description from their book, which is expressive of Perelman and Olbrechts-Tyteca's position:

Suasive Iterations

Unlike political and legal debates, real contests in which two opponents sought to gain the adherence . . . of an audience . . . epideictic speeches had nothing to do with all that. A single orator . . . made a speech, which no one opposed, on topics which are apparently uncontroversial and without practical consequences. . . . [The audience] merely played the part of spectators. After listening to the speaker, they merely applauded and went away. . . . [The] most visible result was to shed luster on their authors. (Perelman and Olbrechts-Tyteca 47-48; Rosenfield 132)

For Perelman and Olbrechts-Tyteca, epideictic's inability to engage agonistically in debate means that it is not as rhetorical as the other two branches of oratory. It is a one-sided display of a speaker's "luster." At best, it serves a pedagogical purpose by "promoting values that are shared in the community," but it is otherwise a sideshow in the domain of rhetoric. (Olbrechts-Tyteca 52; Rosenfield 132)

Countering the marginalization of epideictic in rhetoric theory, Rosenfield returns to Aristotle, who coined the term. In his *Rhetoric*, Aristotle distinguishes epideictic from encomium in the following way:

Now praise [radiance] is language that sets forth greatness of virtue [excellence]; hence it is necessary to show that a man's actions are virtuous. But encomium deals with achievements—all attendant circumstances, such as noble birth and education, merely conduce to persuasion [belief]. (Aristotle 101; Rosenfield 134)

The distinction, Rosenfield explains, is easily lost on a modern scholar. In the ancient world, there was a difference between an individual's accomplishments and the excellence of the act itself. In other words, acts and objects in the real world had a truth all their own—a truth that could be illuminated through speech. Epideictic was Aristotle's term for a speech that expressed that truth:

The pragmatic orientation of our society makes it natural to confuse recognition and valuation. . . . For the Greeks, acknowledgment reaffirmed the virtue, goodness, the quality inherent in object or deed; extravagant praise or boastfulness was confined to panegyric and diatribe, and was not especially prized. (Rosenfield 134-135)

Epideictic was the way in which a rhetor could acknowledge the radiance of Being, and the way by which an audience could witness and appreciate its luminosity.

For/Get the Digital (and Ditch the Umbrella)

When we casuistically stretch epideictic from its linguistic and oratorical bases to the transductive and everted circumstances of the new computing era, the rhetorical value of projects like "Rain Room" emerges. The
suasive value of projects like "Rain Room" is in their ability to illuminate a
previously undisclosed truth about Being. When a rhetor uses physical computing technologies to fold some of the virtual into the real, everting it, she
engages in an act of persuasion associated with epideictic. The feelings of
joy and wonder that participants expressed after experiencing "Rain Room"
are an indication of success. The work may not seem rhetorical because it is
not discursive, but it is a reality-altering event that illuminates or uncon-
ceals some truth for its audience.

In sum, eversion is rhetorical because of its reality-altering effects,
and it is suasive because it participates in the kind of epideictic display that
Rosenfield established. But how can the technical process of transduction—
of energy conversion—be theorized as rhetorical, too? How, for example,
can the numerical representation of the analog flow of electricity across
a sensor be valued rhetorically? The answer to that question brings us to
the third candidate for casuistic stretching, Richard E. Lanham's theory of
allegorical style in *Analyzing Prose*. Like Rosenfield's contribution, Lanham's
stylistic theory needs to be stretched beyond its basis in language and prose
writing. Once that is done, his approach to style helps us reconcile the process of transduction with stylistic innovation.

In *Analyzing Prose*, Lanham argues that when a syntactical pattern becomes "so pronounced" that it communicates a meaning over and above the
content of the narrative or argument with which it is associated, it has become allegorical (30). In other words, when the stylistic form in prose writing rises above the content that it conventionally serves, it has the potential
to communicate something extra-linguistic, something akin to a rhythm or
cadence. That rhythm or cadence is the expression of an allegorized style
that can be used to communicate something outside the content of the narrative or argument—a feeling, concept, or way of being.

Lanham's first example of allegorical style is based on his reading of
a passage from Ernest Hemingway's *A Farewell to Arms*. He claims that Hemingway's style has "come to be *about* connection, *about* a refusal to subordinate"
(30). Hemingway recounts,

> I rode to Gorizia from Udine on a camion. We passed other camions
> on the road and I looked at the country. The mulberry trees were bare
> and the fields were brown. There were wet dead leaves on the road
> from rows of bare trees and men were working on the road, tamping
> stone in the ruts from piles of crushed stone along the side of the road

between the trees. We saw the town with a mist over it that cut off the mountains. *We crossed the river and I saw that it was running high. It had been raining in the mountains.* We came into the town past the factories and then the houses and villas and I saw that many more houses had been hit. On a narrow street we passed a British Red Cross ambulance. The driver wore a cap and his face was thin and very tanned. I did not know him. (qtd. in Lanham 30; my emphasis)

Lanham claims that Hemingway's paratactical style rises above the content of the story. A paratactical style is one in which the connections among the objects, events, and people are left open to interpretation. In other words, they are allowed to exist on the same plane of meaningfulness. The mulberry trees, the men working on the road, and the Red Cross ambulance are equal in value.

Lanham points to the sentence italicized above, noting that the conspicuous absence of "because" is an example of the extent to which Hemingway's style rises above the storyline. Lanham writes, "The obvious 'Because it had been raining in the mountains, the river was running high,' Hemingway declines to elaborate" (30). He concludes, "When a syntactic pattern becomes so pronounced as this, we suspect that the syntax has become allegorical" (30).

Lanham's interpretation of Hemingway's passage focuses on an allegorized meaning, but style can be used to allegorize many things, including an ethos, a feeling, or an ambient state. For example, the paratactical style in Cormac McCarthy's *The Road,* which resembles Hemingway's, allegorizes both a feeling of despondency and the experience of a world reduced to a series of irreconcilably broken and abandoned moments. McCarthy's narrator states,

He let himself in through the kitchen. Trash in the floor, old newsprint. China in a breakfront, cups hanging from their hooks. He went down the hallway and stood in the door to the parlor. There was an antique pump organ in the corner. A television set. Cheap stuffed furniture together with an old handmade cherrywood chifferobe. He climbed the stairs and walked through the bedrooms. Everything covered with ash. (18-19)

Contributing to the allegorized feeling and ambience mentioned above are the interrelated anaphoric and verbal styles: "He let," "He went," "He climbed." And, whereas Hemingway's paratactical style is polysyndentic (numerous conjunctions, such as "and"), McCarthy's asyndentic style accomplishes the same thing. Considering how much the two styles resemble

For/Get the Digital (and Ditch the Umbrella)

each other, we might say that Hemingway's style allegorizes some of the despondency or exhaustion that attends a war zone.

An important conclusion to draw from Lanham's theory of allegorical style is that the schemes within the canon of style, not the tropes, are the technological basis of allegorization in prose. In other words, an allegorical style is not a case of metaphorical extension; rather, it is an extension of schemes. The website *Silva Rhetoricae* defines tropes as "artful deviation[s] from the ordinary or principal meaning of a word." Schemes, on the other hand, are defined as the "artful deviation from the ordinary arrangement of words" ("Trope," "Scheme"). When a rhetor introduces one or more schemes into a discourse, she introduces a rhythm or cadence that acts as a conductor for feeling, ambience, ethos, or meaning. That rhythm or cadence is a type of transducer avant la lettre. When an orator builds a feeling of climax in her audience by repeating an opening word or phrase (anaphora), she has transduced that energy through a deviant use of language. The deviant order of words is a conduit for a transfer of energy, for a transduction that alters reality. The schemes comprising an allegorized style are the bases for transduction in the discursive or linguistic context in which rhetoric is conventionally theorized and practiced.

In an era of physical computing, the transducers—the sensors, actuators, and other types—are casuistically stretched cousins of the schemes. Whereas language-based schemes are defined by the rearrangement of words and letters, transducers rearrange the flow and form of energy. When transducers are used in the service of altering or everting a conventional structure of feeling, they achieve their goal first by converting energy from one form to another. Once a form of conversion is established, the potential for a suasive eversion of an event-space follows.

Distant Writing

Thus far, I have focused on some of the possibilities for a rhetorical approach to physical computing. For digital writers, the opportunities are considerable, too, but they are based on a somewhat radical break from the alphabetic tradition. In Chapter 5, I call for a distant approach to writing. Distant writing is a transductive approach to composition in an era of physical computing partly inspired by Franco Moretti's call for distant reading strategies in the digital humanities. For over a decade, Moretti has been arguing that, in an era of large, digitized corpuses of literary texts (e.g., Google Books and digital libraries like the Hathi Trust), literary scholars' persistent reliance on the close reading of texts is the wrong scale at which to pursue research questions. In place of close reading, Moretti calls for a computationally-driven approach. Moretti writes, "distance is . . . not an obstacle, but *a specific form of knowledge*: fewer elements, hence a sharper sense of their overall interconnection. Shapes, relations, structures. Forms. Models" (1, italics in original). The large-scale patterns of textual meaning discovered by software will be the basis for new research questions, literary theories, and more. At the posthuman scales at which literary works exist now, close reading misses the forest for the trees. With distance, a new proximity emerges, leading to patterns until now long out of reach.

The inspirational point of comparison between Moretti's distant reading and my proposed distant writing is that the latter represents a break from the *logocentric* proximity of writing to speech. Conventionally, writing is defined as a representational technology in the service of speech, and its value is its approximation to phonetic thought. But historically, writing has been defined in far broader terms. In Ancient Greek and Egyptian, and up through the sixteenth century, writing was a term more broadly applied to line-making practices including drawing, etching, scratching, and tracing. In an era of physical computing in which such inscriptive practices are both essential and non-alphabetic, the challenge before us is to make the leap toward a new way of thinking about writing—to distance ourselves from what linguist Roy Harris has called the "tyranny of the alphabet" (29). In an era of physical computing, writing with electricity is an essential part of the transductive process, but it is not alphabetic; rather, it involves the line-making process of wiring various kinds of components together into circuits. Drawing lines of electricity across components in a physical computing project is not alphabetic, but it is a species of (transductive) writing.

As I explain in Chapter 5, the notion that the twenty-six line drawings comprising our alphabet represent the distinct sounds of speech does not hold up under scrutiny. Language is not an atomized set of sounds, and the alphabet does not represent comprehensively all of the sounds of speech. As linguist H. Paul explains, "[speech] is essentially a continuous series of infinitely numerous sounds, and alphabetical symbols do no more than bring out certain characteristic points of this series in an imperfect way" (qtd in Harris 39). In other words, the twenty-six line drawings comprising the alphabet are representative of inflection points along a continuous, multidimensional event-stream. Those line drawings have proven their worth as a mark-up system, but they do not capture or transduce all of the energy associated with the analog flow of speech.

A recognition of the limits of the alphabet offer writing theorists the opportunity to broaden their notion of what writing can be; the limits point to a broader definitional scope. If we casuistically stretch the conventional description of writing, redescribing it as a mark-up system for transducing some of the analog flow of speech, and if we are willing to say that,

For/Get the Digital (and Ditch the Umbrella)

as a transductive technology, it could be expanded to convert other energy flows beyond those associated with speech, then there is an opportunity to both "distance" writing from its naturalized relationship with speech and to reconnect writing to its broader historical definition. Writing as the practice of making lines can take many forms and serve many ends. One powerful way in which it has been deployed is to transduce speech, but in an era of physical computing, transductive or distant writing connects our understanding of writing to its historical past via the circuits a writer designs to work with electricity.

Chapters

In Chapter 2, "A Transductive Science of the Concrete," I present a method for digital stylistic invention related to Cramer's and Levi-Strauss's theories of computation and creativity. The goal of the method is to discover new species of (transductive) flowers of rhetoric based on specific microtechnologies and microprocesses. The new post-PC era demands an approach to digital rhetorical invention that is radically materialist. What this means is that we need to turn explicitly to the microtechnologies and computational processes on which a transductive theory of rhetoric can be built.

The inventional method presented in Chapter 2 includes the following steps: 1) discover the intertextual dimensions of a specific technology or process; 2) map out the low-level transductive possibilities of the technology or process; and 3) discover ways in which to allegorize the technology based on its low-level affordances and constraints. Taken together, the method is one of stylistic allegorization. In *Analyzing Prose*, Richard Lanham writes about several styles that rise to the level of allegory. When style becomes allegorical, it rises above the text that it conventionally supports. The ability to allegorize microtechnologies and microprocesses is the way in which a new flowerbed of style serving invention can be grown.

The focus of Chapter 3, "Onto-Allegories for the 'Great Outdoors,'" is a response to the ideal of peaceful or invisible computing developed under the banner of ubiquitous computing (ubicomp). First theorized by Mark Weiser and his research group at XEROX Parc in the 1990s, ubicomp was an emerging approach to popular computing that was meant to respond to the following problem: humanity was being overwhelmed by noisy, demanding (personal) computers. Moreover, personal computers were too limited to engage with what Adam Greenfield calls the interstitial moments in our lives, such as looking for our keys, wondering which way to commute home, and being reminded to run errands. Ubicomp is an approach to computing that is designed to support the seemingly trivial questions and issues on our way to the main events in our day. It is an approach to computing in which distributed computational processes serve us constantly but peripherally. Weiser once wrote, "The most profound technologies are those that disappear. They weave themselves into the fabric of everyday life until they are indistinguishable from it" (66). Ubicomp promises an even more intimate association with computation than the PC, but in ways that are largely invisible to us.

From a rhetorical standpoint, there are two problems with this call for peaceful, invisible computing. The first is the limited range of rhetorical appeal in which "invisible" technologies can engage. Ubicomp as theorized by Weiser resembles the approach to rhetoric that Richard Lanham once associated with the three anti-rhetorical ideals of clarity, brevity, and sincerity, or the CBS style. A CBS style in computing inadvertently perpetuates a distrust of rhetoric in the new computational era, which limits the range of appeal to which we could otherwise engage; moreover, it disconnects digital rhetoric from the critical traditions to which it has been engaged in the past century. The second problem with a call for "invisible" computing is that it limits the extent to which we might foreground specific microtechnologies and processes in order to experiment with them.

With these issues in mind, Chapter 3 borrows from recent work in object-oriented philosophy, calling on digital rhetors to leave the correlationist confines of ubicomp for the wilderness of invention and experimentation. The project at the center of the chapter is intended to demonstrate how we might disturb the peace to which ubicomp aspires. Based on Ian Bogost's chapter-length discussion of ontography, I argue that we can use his taxonomy to develop projects that foreground the object-ness of ubicomp 'wares, which might otherwise evade our critical and experimental view.

The argument in Chapter 4, "Plumbing the Paradoxical Depths," is based on some of my experiments with Microsoft's *Kinect* sensor. In immersive computing environments in which visual and aural feedback can influence a participant's experience of their spatio-temporal relations to their bodies, there is an opportunity to revitalize and extend the largely-forgotten focus on corporeal performance, posture, and gesture in the canon of delivery. The canon of delivery has gone through something of a revival in digital media, but the focus has been on media as delivery systems, interfaces, and protocols. The body is still largely absent from the resurgent interest in the lost canon. With sensors like Microsoft's *Kinect*, it is now possible to augment the digital canon of delivery with corporeal experimentations.

Inspired by Jose Gil's Deleuzian approach to studying the "paradoxical" space-time of dancers' bodies, and by Anna Munster's explorations of emerging materialities at the intersection of the digital and analog, I propose that we redefine the canon of (digital) delivery as an inventional

For/Get the Digital (and Ditch the Umbrella)

framework. In the immersive computing environments in which the *Kinect* is running, the following framework can be established as a basis for invention: a *Kinect* sensor is used to map the space in real-time; the data from that space is transduced with algorithms that are designed to change the visual and aural feedback in the space; the feedback becomes an implicit interface through which new experiences of the body can be established.

In Chapter 5, "A Call for Distant (Transductive) Writing," I argue for an approach to writing that returns us to its 'pre-alphabetic' status as a way of making lines. Working from Roy Harris's and Tim Ingold's writing theories, I call for what I described earlier as a distant approach to writing, which is a transductive form of writing as line making. When even traditional writing is redefined as a transductive technology, an opportunity emerges to develop new branches of transductive writing that operate at a distance from speech and phonetic thought.

In Chapter 6, I conclude by developing connections between two issues. The first is related to the need to move beyond the PC era. Spike Jonze's film *Her* is used to foreground the challenges that are involved. The film seems to promote a futuristic, post-PC culture—but it becomes apparent that the NUI-based technologies depicted in the film serve an all-too-familiar PC era. After a short analysis of the climactic scene, which can be related to the post-correlationist argument in Chapter 3, I push for a move beyond personal computing in rhetoric and writing. In order to innovate in the new era of physical computing, I argue that the bookishness of the PC era—and, along with it, the ethos of Theodore—must be left behind.

The second issue is the exigence to move beyond what Marshall McLuhan might have called the "gadget loving" phase in physical computing, by recognizing the supportive role these kinds of projects represent rhetorically. Realizing that the project, itself, is a complex, rhetorical appeal serving an implicit or explicit claim, is an essential first step toward integrating this kind of work into our discipline. On the surface, digital rhetors and writers may be designing circuits, writing code, and transducing the analog to the digital and back, but all of these practices are a technical means to a rhetorical end: moving audiences.

Transductive Technologies

An important feature of *Suasive Iterations* is the inclusion of four original physical computing projects, which are meant to extend the scholarly topics and discussions developed in the book. At the end of Chapters 2, 3, 4, and 5 are shorter half-chapters designated by a ".5." Each of those half chapters offer an overview of the project as well as a link to a website where how-to videos, technical specifications, downloadable code, and circuit designs are available. The projects in each of the half chapters foreground the transductive potential of the technologies on which each project is based. In other words, the projects are designed as heuristics for invention.

As a way of making explicit these heuristics for invention, a visualization dashboard accompanies each project. The dashboards are meant to underscore the ways in which transduction can be creatively pursued in order to stylistically allegorize the data to which you have access. Figure 7, for example, shows the visualization dashboard developed for the project in Chapter 4.5.

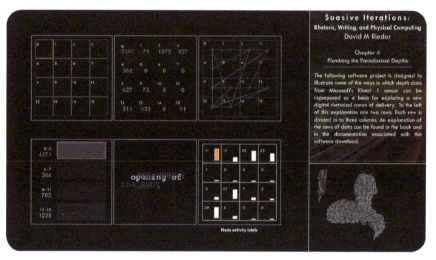

Figure 7. Visualization dashboard for Chapter 4.5.

There are five technologies on which the four physical computing projects are based. The first is the Arduino microcontroller (see Figure 8). The Arduino is a small computer that fits in the palm of your hand. It doesn't come with a screen, keyboard or mouse because it is not a part of the PC era. What it does come with is a series of digital and analog pins with which you can read or "write" electrical energy.

For/Get the Digital (and Ditch the Umbrella)

Figure 8. Arduino UNO. Photo credit: SparkFun Electronics.

The Arduino was first developed in 2005 by faculty and graduate students in at the Interaction Design Institute in Ivrea, Italy. It has since become a cornerstone in physical computing work and the open hardware movement because its design is open, it is inexpensive, and it is easy to program. As an indication of its popularity, in 2010, over 130,000 Arduinos had been sold. There are over 15 million hits per month on the Arduino. cc website, or approximately 600,000 hits each day. In the United States, thanks to companies like SparkFun and AdaFruit Industries, who both supply Arduino boards and the dozens of compatible sensors, actuators, and shields that are available, Arduino has become a near universal platform for prototyping projects. The microcontroller is the basis of the projects in Chapter 2.5.

The second technology is the Arduino-based Touch Board by Bare Conductive.

Figure 9. Bare Conductive's Touch Board with conductive paint. Photo credit: Bare Conductive.

The Touch Board is based on a 12-input capacitive touch sensor (or cap sensor). Cap sensors are ubiquitous in today's post-PC world; most touch screens are based on this technology. In Figure 9 above, several of the board's inputs are extended with the use of conductive paint, which makes it possible to repurpose objects, walls, and even skin into a sensory input.

The third technology is Microsoft's first *Kinect*, which was released in December 2010 as a peripheral for the XBOX 360 gaming and entertainment system. Within a month, it had been "hacked" by two groups. Those two hacks would lead to an explosion of experimental work based on the sensory capabilities of the device. Based in part on the *Kinect*'s popularity as an open platform for academics, businesses, artists, and DIYers, Microsoft put out an official software development kit (SDK), so developers could work toward some of the same ends.

For/Get the Digital (and Ditch the Umbrella)

Figure 10. Front-facing view of partially disassembled *Kinect*.

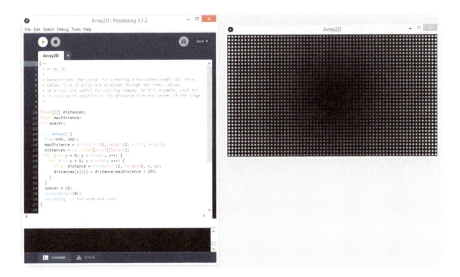

Figure 11. On the left, Processing's Integrated Development Environment (IDE). On the right, the display window with the project generated by the code in the IDE.

The last two technologies are a pair of interrelated programming languages, Processing and the Arduino language. One or both of these languages are an integral part of all four projects. Processing was initially developed by two MIT graduate students, Ben Fry and Casey Reas. As it has grown in popularity, dozens of developers have been involved in its evolution. It was released in 2001, and it has since become one of the most popular "high-level" languages for both learning and practicing a wide range of computationally driven, creative projects. It is an open language, and is available for Windows, Macintosh, and Linux.

Although the Arduino language is based on the languages C and C++, it was designed as a complement to Processing. Arduino is the language with which you program the microcontroller of the same name. When the two languages are combined in a project, it means that the vast range of data that can be accessed through a PC or smartphone can be extended to the Arduino, and that all of the sensory data from the analog world with which the Arduino interacts can be imported to Processing. These two languages are an example of the way in which the analog and digital can be folded together. In combination, they make the transductive process relatively easy to explore.

2 Transduction and Allegorized Style

Rhetoric is at its best when its practices and theory are explicitly engaged with the materialities comprising the cutting edge of suasive possibilities. When addressing audiences for whom the era of physical computing is a cutting-edge framework, rhetoricians (and writers) must discover the available means of transduction, in order to understand how to creatively and suasively evert an interactive space. Since eversion is based on the use of sensors and actuators to fold together aspects of the virtual/digital and analog/real, an inventional approach based in style that begins with those components is essential because those components are the bases of a new, casuistically stretched approach to the "flowers" of rhetoric.

In rhetoric, there is a long tradition of calling the tropes and schemes comprising the figures of speech the flowers of rhetoric. Traditionally, the flowers are language-based ways in which to transform (or transduce) the sounds, rhythms, relationships, and meanings of words toward suasive ends. If we characterize the discovery of new flowers as a process of botanization, then, as a rhetor learns how to "botanize" the transductive microcomponents on which the new era is based—identifying their affordances and constraints, and then cataloging the many ways in which the data associated with them can be transduced and allegorized—she will have taken an important step forward toward the establishment of a new canon of stylistic invention.

The approach to stylistic allegorization developed in this book begins with a casuistic stretching of Richard Lanham's analysis of prose style in *Analyzing Prose*. In Chapter 1, I explained that, for Lanham, a style has become allegorical when it rises above the content of the narrative or argument with which it is associated. Lanham's first example of an allegorical style is from his analysis of a passage from Ernest Hemingway's *A Farewell to Arms*. In that passage, Hemingway's use of parataxis and polysyndeton is "so pronounced" that it "has become allegorical, has come to be *about* connection, *about* a refusal to subordinate" (30). One more of Lanham's examples of allegorical prose style is from Henry James's *The Wings of the Dove*. In the following excerpt, Lanham colorizes red and adds parentheses around the stylistic elements that contribute to the allegorization of an equivocating thought process:

Suasive Iterations

. . . and the soreness and the shame were less as he let himself, (with the help of the conditions about him), regard it as serious. It was born, (for that matter), partly of the conditions, (those conditions that Kate had (so almost insolently) braved), had been willing, (without a pang,) to see him ridiculously—(ridiculously (so far as just complacently))—exposed to. (Lanham 57, his emphasis)

The parentheses and colored words are Lanham's way of highlighting the parenthetical style in the passage, which creates a "dominant seesaw rhythm" (59). The seesaw rhythm, Lanham explains, contributes to a style that "has become allegorical, a style about the hesitation and qualification it creates" (59). A stylistic characteristic of someone who is equivocating can include interjections of worries and fears in the flow of thought, and those interjections can be represented allegorically in prose by a parenthetical style.

Lanham's allegorical analyses are not limited to prose style. He also cites several examples of "typographical allegory," including Laurence Sterne's experimental use of dashes, asterisks, italics, and line drawings, John Cage's experiments with typography and page layout in compositions such as "Silence," and Kenneth Burke's flowerishes (87-94). All three are compelling examples of writers and artists who visually change the size, shape, position, and boldness of type in order to allegorize an idea or feeling.

As Lanham expands the scope of allegorical style beyond prose to include typographical experiments, it is easier to imagine a casuistic stretching of his approach that extends to the digital era. One digital example that fits his definition of allegorized style is Shelley Jackson's hypertext story, *Patchwork Girl*.

Transduction and Allegorized Style

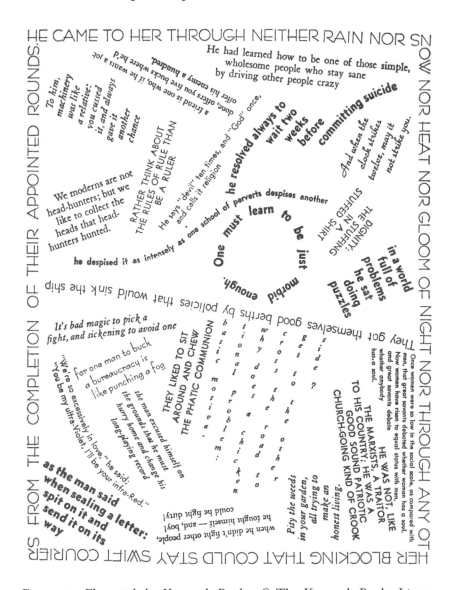

Figure 12. Flowerish by Kenneth Burke. © The Kenneth Burke Literary Trust. Used by permission.

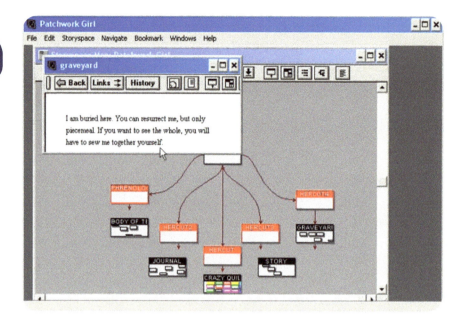

Figure 13. Screen shot from Patchwork Girl. Photo credit: James Barrett.

Jackson uses the hypertextual medium to allegorize the protagonist's "schizophrenic" reality. The difficulties that the reader experiences unifying the parts of the story are a by-product of her style of linking. Jackson's style is an artful deviation from the conventional order of a linear narrative. As a reader engages with Jackson's work, they experience some of the confusion and frustration that her protagonist experiences within the narrative.

Another digital example of stylistic allegorization is "Crushed Under Sodium Lights," by Dave Bevan and Brendan Dawes (see Figure 14 below). Published in *Born Magazine* in 2002, it persists as a compelling example of Flash-based digital poetry. The project transduces a user's mouse movements across the x and y axes of the screen to allegorize some of the experience and ambience of a city night. The poem is divided among eight screens, and each screen-as-stanza is performed against an image of city life under the sodium streetlights that illuminate it. Sounds, words, and images swirl and fade in transduced synchronization with the movements of the mouse. The project offers users the chance to playback their recorded mouse movements, so they can watch what they have participated in allegorizing.

Transduction and Allegorized Style

Figure 14. Screen capture of "Crushed Under Sodium Lights." Photo credit: Dave Bevan and Brendan Dawes.

A casuistically-stretched, allegorized style is not confined to screen-based works, either. In the post-PC era, art installations like "Rain Room" demonstrate how transductive technologies can be used to allegorize an experience, feeling, or concept. Projects like "Rain Room" are essentially style machines. Their successes are based on a stylistic allegorization of participation, which is in turn based on transductions of analog data representative of those engagements. As I explained in Chapter 1, one of the transductive bases of "Rain Room" is the suite of depth cameras. In order to generate the gap or distance between a participant and the simulated rainfall, the 3D depth data must be transduced and reconciled with the two-dimensional grid of water valves overhead.

If we are willing to casuistically stretch the stylistic schemes beyond their linguistic origins and toward the era of physical computing in which "Rain Room" operates, an opportunity presents itself to botanize the computationally-derived gap between a participant and the rainfall as the effect of a new type of style. For example, a digital rhetorician could think of the gap as a new species of stylistic interruption. The website *Silva Rhetoricae* associates the schemes of interruption with grammatical disruptions, or with disruptions in "the emotional flow of discourse" ("Figures of Interruption"). Clearly, the transduced gap in the rainfall is not a grammatical or discursive disruption; nonetheless, it is a disruptive technology serving a stylistically allegorical, rhetorical end.

Suasive Iterations

A Transductive Science of the Concrete

For rhetors who want to engage in the process of discovery—to botanize the sensors and actuators comprising the new flowerbed of stylistic invention—experimentation is an important first step. How do we conceptualize the process? How do we proceed? The remainder of this chapter answers those questions. I begin with a Nietzschean call to overturn one of the "truths" of the new era—a truth that serves the end user but not the inventor. Then, I develop a connection between Massimo Banzi's call to tinker and Claude Levi-Strauss's theory of bricolage and his "science of the concrete" (Levi-Strauss 1). Massimo's and Levi-Strauss's works are meant to offer some conceptual backing for a process of transductive invention, which, inspired by Levi-Strauss's "science of the concrete," can then be called a *transductive* science of the concrete. From there, I introduce Florian Cramer's provocative redescription of the historical moment when computational thinking was born in the West. Cramer argues that computational thought can be traced back historically to the Middle Ages, and that the roots of computational thinking, which coalesce in the Middle Ages, reach back millennia (Cramer 122).

With the connections among Nietzsche, Banzi, Levi-Strauss and Cramer behind us, the last part of the chapter is an in-depth, annotated, seven-step process for transducing and allegorizing sensory data. This inventional process is an answer to the question, "How to we proceed?," and it will be based on Analog Device's ADXL335 triple-axis MEMS accelerometer, which SparkFun sells on a breakout board for prototyping. The same sensor will be the basis for the project in Chapter 2.5.

Figure 15. ADXL335 accelerometer. Photo credit: SparkFun Electronics.

Transduction and Allegorized Style

Nietzschean Truths Are *Everyware*

The Nietzschean critique of truth has newfound relevance in an era that Adam Greenfield calls *everyware*. For Greenfield, everyware is a term that describes generally the way in which physical computing technologies are "invisibly present" in users' everyday lives. Greenfield writes, "there are powerful informatics underlying the apparent simplicity of the experience, but they never break the surface of awareness: things Just Work" (36). From the standpoint of experimentation, this "truth" of the new era will have to be overturned—and Nietzsche's argument against truth is a provocative and inspiring call to invention.

In the following excerpt from his essay, "On Truth and Lies in a Non-Moral Sense," Nietzsche offers a definition of truth that calls into question the face value of established values and beliefs:

> What, then, is truth? A mobile army of metaphors, metonyms, and anthropomorphisms—in short, a sum of human relations which have been enhanced, transposed, and embellished poetically and rhetorically, and which after long use seem firm, canonical, and obligatory to a people: truths are illusions about which one has forgotten that this is what they are; metaphors which are worn out and without sensuous power; coins which have lost their pictures and now matter only as metal, no longer as coins. (43)

Nietzsche's definition of truth is a mnemonic dynamic born of obligation and time-honored beliefs. It is a stop-gap to the wildness of life in language. For Nietzsche, innovation begins in the flowerbeds of rhetorical style and invention, where human social relations are in constant flux. But over time, the rich and sensuous forces comprising those metaphors, metonyms, and anthropomorphisms lose face and are forgotten. The transductive currency of Nietsche's coins are erased by tradition and obligation. Truth is a mnemonic relation, a stitch in time. Nietzsche describes truth as "illusions about which one has forgotten that is what they are" (44).

The importance of Nietzsche's argument is that, over the millennia, rhetoric has been a transgressive force. It has transgressed ritual, tradition, and obligation in order to move audiences. Truths, or stitches in time, are pulled apart, their idiosyncratic dynamics uncovered in order to employ their sensuous powers toward suasive ends. The flowers of rhetoric are a case in point. The scores of tropes and schemes comprising the linguistic canon of style are a historical ledger of the ways in which human relations are expressed in language, as well as the means through which human relations can be elicited to move audiences.

Suasive Iterations

Nearly a century after Nietzsche's essay was published, an army of microtechnologies associated with the new era of physical computing is establishing itself as a new kind of faceless truth. They are *everyware,* a smart technology designed to mask the sensuous dance with which they are engaged. In the following quote, Greenfield describes a technology that resembles the faceless coins about which Nietzsche wrote:

> Household objects from shower stalls to coffee pots are reimagined as places where facts about the world can be gathered, considered, and acted upon. And all the familiar rituals of daily life . . . are remade as an intricate dance of information about ourselves, the state of the external world, and the options available to us at any given moment. In all of these scenarios, there are powerful informatics underlying the apparent simplicity of the experience, but they never breach the surface of awareness. (1)

If in the new era of physical computing, the sensors, actuators, and cloud-based algorithmic processes on which the above-described "dance of information" is based constitute the new flowerbed of stylistic invention, then rhetoric is faced with a challenge. In order to discover the available means of transductive suasion, rhetors will have to breach the surface of awareness, the illusion of truth. These microcomponents and microprocesses are the basis for an entirely new mobile army of tropes and schemes. But learning how to botanize them, and then how to graft them toward new suasive ends, is a challenge. At the preliminary stages of invention, experimentation is essential—but how can experimentation be theorized and understood? The answer to that question is epitomized by both Massimo Banzi's tinkerer and Claude Levi-Strauss's *bricoleur*. Their two avatars engage in a form of experimentation that Levi-Strauss might have called a "science of the concrete."

Massimo Banzi is one the co-founding developers of Arduino. In his book, *Getting Started with Arduino*, he outlines an 8-part heuristic for invention that he calls "The Arduino Way." In the following excerpt, Banzi underscores the importance of tinkering as an open-ended approach to invention:

> Classic engineering relies on a strict process for getting from A to B; the Arduino Way delights in the possibility of getting lost on the way and finding C instead. This is the tinkering process that we are so fond of—playing with the medium in an open-ended way and finding the unexpected. (5)

Transduction and Allegorized Style

Tinkering is an informal but well-documented way of discovering the available means of transduction in a component or device. Old or new components and processes are played with in order to identify their potential for creative and suasive engagement. To borrow from Nietzsche's critique, tinkering is a way in which to defamiliarize a component's truth, i.e., the limited ways in which the component is conventionally used. The tinkerer and Levi-Strauss's *bricoleur* epitomize a way forward.

In his chapter titled "Science of the Concrete," published in *The Savage Mind*, Levi-Strauss offers a sophisticated backdrop against which to appreciate the role of tinkering as a formal process of discovery and engagement—one that can be traced back millennia. He begins with a rebuttal against the modern assumption that early historical practices associated with magic and myth were unsophisticated and primitive. Levi-Strauss counters that these early practices and systematic ways of thinking should be recognized as a viable, parallel approach to science alongside the modern incarnation. They are not primitive; rather, they exist prior to the modern approaches against which the past is defined. Levi-Strauss argues, "Magical thought is not to be regarded as a beginning, a rudiment, a sketch, a part of a whole which has not yet materialized. It forms a well-articulated system, and is in this respect independent of that other system which constitutes science" (13). Magic and science both require "the same sort of mental operations," for which reason they do not differ in kind. No doubt, modern science has proven to be more successful at determining the causes of phenomena, but the two are both ordered, reasoned, sophisticated systems of thought. Magical thought should not be dismissed.

The basic difference between the two is their proximity to the sensible world. Modern science operates at a remove from nature, whereas magical thought is directly engaged with its smells, colors, and textures. Whereas modern science will endeavor to abstract from a smell or color a chemical equation or formula, the neolithic approach engages directly with them. Smells and colors are cataloged and associated in a grand scheme of causality of which all of nature is an expression. It is due to the latter's proximity to nature that Levi-Strauss calls magical or neolithic thought a "science of the concrete." The focus on the sensible is an implicit call to focus radically on the materialities on which the new era of physical computing is based.

In defense of the counter-argument that magical thought does not accurately identify the causes on which nature is based, Levi-Strauss rebuts, "Any classification is superior to chaos and even a classification at the level of sensible properties is a step toward rational ordering" (12). Magical thought may not identify the causes behind nature's order as accurately as does modern science, but it is a sophisticated system of ordering the world;

moreover, its conclusions are sometimes accurate. The point is that an inventional process that begins with effects rather than causes can lead serendipitously to highly productive ends.

In order to understand the "logic" on which magical thought is based, James G. Fraser's analysis is often cited. In fact, Levi-Strauss cites it, too. In *The Golden Bough*, Fraser explains that magical thought and practice is divided between two distinct principles or laws. Fraser introduces them as follows: "First, that like produces like, or that an effect resembles its cause; and, second, that things which have once been in contact with each other continue to act on each other at a distance after the physical contact has been severed" (12). Fraser goes on to call the first principle the Law of Similarity; the second is the Law of Contagion. Arising from the first is the belief that an effect can be produced by imitation, for which reason the practice associated with it is called homoeopathic or imitative magic. From the second is derived the belief that manipulating a material object with which someone once had contact will have an effect on her. The second belief is associated with contagious magic.

It is worth noting that Fraser characterizes magic as an art, not a science: "the very idea of science is lacking in [primitive man's] undeveloped mind" (13). Apparently, Fraser is one of the scholars against whom Levi-Strauss was writing.

Over and above the need to further define what magical thinking was in practice, the main reason I cite Fraser's laws of magic is that it has been associated with stylistic invention. In his study of aphasia titled "Two Aspects of Language and Two Types of Aphasic Disturbances," linguist Roman Jakobson argues that all instances of aphasic events can be associated with one of two disorders: similarity disorders and contiguity disorders. Influenced by Fraser's analysis of magic, Jakobson associates the two disorders with his theory of two axes of choice and selection in language. The first order resembles Fraser's law of similarity, and the second resembles Fraser's law of contagion.

Jakobson introduces the connection to stylistic invention when he relates the two axes to the tropes, metaphor and metonymy. According to Jakobson, metaphor is an expression of similarity. Metonymy is an expression of contiguity. These two tropes are the basis for Jakobson's "bipolar" theory of language. Applying Jakobson's theories to Fraser's two principles of laws, we can speculate that magical thought is an expression of the bipolarity of language, which is based on the two interrelated dynamics of metaphorical and metonymic relations. We can speculate even further that Levi-Strauss's analysis of magical thinking is an elaboration on this bipolar, tropological dynamic.

Transduction and Allegorized Style

Turning back to his discussion of the science of the concrete, Levi-Strauss points to a modern-day avatar of the neolithic science of the concrete, the *bricoleur*. There is no equivalent for the French term in English, but two popular translations are "Jack of all trades" and tinkerer. In order to appreciate Levi-Strauss's comparison, there is a point worth mentioning that is related to his discussion of magical thought. According to Levi-Strauss, magic and myth are two interrelated sides of the same coin. Magical thought operates on what he calls the "technical plane," while myths operate on the speculative or intellectual plane. Whereas magical thought is action-oriented, which means that its practices are meant to produce something new in the world, myth's role is mnemonic. The value of myths is "to preserve until the present time the remains of methods of observation and reflection" related to magical practices (11). The "logic" of the two is similar, but the outcomes are different.

Since the bricoleur is not engaged in magic, Levi-Strauss argues that the link between the science of the concrete and the bricoleur is through myth: "Mythical thought is a kind of intellectual 'bricolage'—which explains the relation which can be perceived between the two" (17). A study of bricolage, then, offers us additional insight into the neolithic age.

The main reason bricolage and mythical thought are related is that they are both constrained by a closed, limited, heterogeneous set of elements that they reuse in clever and creative ways. In the following excerpt, Levi-Strauss describes the "universe" in which the bricoleur operates:

> [The *bricoleur*'s] universe of instruments is closed and the rules of his game are always to make do with 'whatever is at hand,' that is to say with a set of tools and materials which is always finite and is also heterogeneous because what it contains bears no relation to the current project, or indeed to any particular project, but is the contingent result of all the occasions there have been to renew or enrich the stock or to maintain it with the remains of previous constructions or destructions. (17)

In American popular culture, television shows like MacGyver and some of the competitive chef shows epitomize the practices of the bricoleur. From a limited set of elements, a seemingly endless range of diverse ends can be achieved. This constrained, creative process is a practical expression of the intellectual operations of mythic thought associated with the science of the concrete.

In contrast to the bricoleur, Levi-Strauss argues that the engineer's repertoire of tools and techniques are defined by the specific project at hand. In this sense, the engineer's "universe of instruments" is open

Suasive Iterations

and forever growing. There are as many different sets of tools as there are projects. Banzi echoes this point in his description of tinkering, which he contrasts with the scientific approach of the engineer. Banzi writes, "Reusing existing technology is one of the best ways of tinkering. Getting cheap toys or old discarded equipment and hacking them to do something new is one of the best ways to get great results" (7). His call to reuse existing technology is an implicit call to work with a limited set of tools that can be repurposed in many different ways. For Banzi, this approach to science, which he calls tinkering, is an invaluable creative process in the framework of physical computing.

With Levi-Strauss's theory of bricolage, magic, and myth in mind, several points can be derived that are related to the development of a transductive science of the concrete. The first is that invention can be valued as a constrained process of creation—one that is based on a closed and limited set of operational units. The operational units can be valued as a nascent repertoire of rhetorical figures, the value of which would relate directly to a new canon of style. Sensors, actuators, and algorithmic processes that have been used in one context, serving one truth, can be repurposed in "extra-moral" ways to serve new ends. Tinkering is an essential way in which to identify the material bases of transductive suasion. Developing the means of transductive suasion requires that we understand the material affordances and constraints of the technologies on which it is based. In order to muster the mobile army of smartifactual units to suasive ends, their material potential must be studied and experimented with.

There is another historical layer in which to wrap the discussion of bricolage, myth, and magic: the wide-ranging, early history of computational thinking and practices that long predate the digital computer. In his book, *Words Made Flesh*, Florian Cramer offers an alternative view of computational thinking that has a direct bearing on both rhetoric and Levi-Strauss's science of the concrete.

In *Words Made Flesh: Code, Culture, Imagination*, Cramer argues that computational practices and thinking long predate the digital revolution. Their origins can be found in two distinct modes of thought and practice that coalesce in the early Middle Ages. The first is magical thought and practice, which Cramer reminds us is a type of executable language or code: "Material creation from the word is an idea central to magic in all cultures; it is precisely what magic spells perform. Magic therefore is, at its core, a technology, serving the rational end of achieving an effect, and being judged by its efficacy" (14-15). Although magical practices have long been discredited as a science, the belief in the generative qualities of language has been persistent throughout the West's history.

Transduction and Allegorized Style

As a poignant example of the persistent interest and belief in the power of magical/executable language in the West, Cramer cites a permutational poem by Brion Gysin and William S. Burroughs that uses a computer to shuffle the opening words from the Gospel of John. The following excerpt features a few lines from the permutation:

IN THE BEGINNING WAS THE WORD

IN THE BEGINNING WAS WORD THE

IN THE BEGINNING WORD THE WAS

IN THE BEGINNING WORD WAS THE

IN THE THE BEGINNING WAS WORD

IN THE THE BEGINNING WORD WAS

IN THE THE WAS BEGINNING WORD

IN THE THE WAS WORD BEGINNING

IN THE THE WORD BEGINNING WAS

IN THE THE WORD WAS BEGINNING

IN THE WAS BEGINNING THE WORD

IN THE WAS BEGINNING WORD THE

(Cramer 17)

Cramer explains that the six words comprising the poem are "shuffled" in accordance with a formal algorithm that was co-developed in the early 1960s with mathematician Ian Sommerville. The algorithm was executed on a Honeywell computer, generating 720 permutations of the opening words from the Gospel. Embodied in this example is an implicit belief in the generative power of (computational) language.

The second mode of thought and practice about which Cramer writes is a belief in the numerical basis of the cosmos. Cramer cites the Pythagoreans as an origin for this belief in the West. He writes,

When Pythagoras discovered the arithmetic principle of the musical octave by splitting the string of a monochord in half, and from that concluded that there was a mathematical harmony to the cosmos, he founded an aesthetic philosophy that closely linked art, science, and nature and whose impact was immense through the Renaissance and beyond. (20)

The belief in a numerical and harmonic order to all of nature and the cosmos persists in various forms today. The belief has become a commonplace, due to the influence of digital technologies in the popular consciousness—from the Human Genome Project, which has helped to establish the commonplace that life is a code, to films like *The Matrix*, at the end of which Neo finally proves that he's "The One" when he can see everything as pure code.

Cramer is quick to point out that neither one of these two practices or beliefs is enough to give rise to computational thinking. Ultimately, the two must coalesce. On the one hand, Pythagorean thinking envisions the world as a numerical code, but it is "not yet a source code and language that instigates processes" (28). Cramer continues, "there is code, but no execution in the code" (28). Magic, on the other hand, "lacks the concept of a formal language because it conflates, through its two modes of similarity and contact, its own language with the objects and subjects involved in its act" (28). But when the two combine, computational thought is born.

Cramer never cites Claude Levi-Strauss's "science of the concrete." The omission is surprising because the two works have a lot in common. Perhaps the reason is that Levi-Strauss contradicts a point on which Cramer relies in Frazer's work. In Frazer's study of magic, Cramer explains that "magical practices tend to cloud their technical and formalist nature, enmeshing themselves with the semantics of the objects and subjects they are intended to affect" (Cramer 18). This is an important point for Cramer because it plays into his claim that computational thought requires a distinct cosmo-numerical view of the world.

If this is the reason, I would counter that while Levi-Strauss does not discriminate between the two originary sources for computational thinking found in Cramer's work, the neolithic science about which he writes is a coalescence of both. The magical/mythical dimensions of neolithic thought imply both an action-oriented approach to language and a view of Nature that resembles a grand, causal scheme of formal associations. For whatever were Cramer's reasons for omitting Levi-Strauss, the figure of the bricoleur would have been a productive addition to his argument.

The tinkerer about whom Banzi writes is exemplary of Cramer's computational culture. Banzi's tinkerer assumes a formal structure to the world in which she hacks her 'wares, and the experimental transductions that she performs in code and circuitry harken back to the age of magic.

In the final chapter of his book, Cramer presents the following definition of software: "Software . . . is a cultural practice made up of (a) algorithms, (b) possibly, but not necessarily in conjunction with imaginary or actual machines, (c) human interaction in a broad sense of any cultural

Transduction and Allegorized Style

appropriation of use, and (d) speculative imagination" (124). He ends his book with a counter-argument against the conventional distinction between "software as immaterial" and "hardware as material" (124). Cramer argues that the distinction falls apart fairly easily under scrutiny. For one, something as abstract and presumably immaterial as an algorithm is "material stored in its coded form"; so, the algorithmic definition of software complicates the conventional distinction (124). In addition to the material bases of algorithms are several more forms of software that exist chiefly in imaginative forms. Cramer cites vaporware, hoax viruses, pseudo-code, artistic forms such as Perl poetry, and some technotexts. Cramer's ultimate point is that software is a broad, cultural category that is ultimately an expression of a long, cultural history of computational thought.

When the history of rhetoric is mapped on to Cramer's argument, it seems possible that rhetoric has been at times in its history a computational enterprise; in some ways, it still is. For one thing, the sophistic belief in the power of language echoes a magical influence within the ancient practice; so, one half of Cramer's theory is present. And many of the suasive techniques associated with invention imply a formal system of relations. That system may not be numerical, but it assumes a complex, causal network in which everything is connected.

The scores of tropes and schemes comprising the canon of style are like tiny machines through which language is transduced toward suasive ends. Rhetoric is not just a science of the concrete. With Cramer's broad definition of computational thought in mind, rhetoric is a transductive, computational science of the concrete.

Botanizing the ADXL 335 MEMS Accelerometer: A Micro-Electromechanical Flower

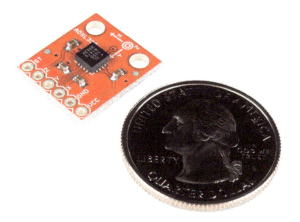

Figure 16. ADXL 335 (the small black square) on a breakout board. Photo credit: SparkFun Electronics.

The ADXL 335 is a 3-axis MEMS accelerometer manufactured by Analog Devices. It has three separate sensors for each of the three dimensions x, y, and z. MEMS is an acronym for micro-electromechanical system. MEMS are characterized by their microscopic size. The ADXL 335 is 4 x 4 x 1.45 millimeters in size, which is something worth considering for a moment. It would fit inside this letter o; nonetheless, it is a tiny machine with moving parts, electrical circuits, a microprocessor, and several other microelectronic technologies, including an analog-to-digital converter (ADC). It is a sophisticated factory of micro-mechanical parts electrical circuitry, and software.

  One of the challenges for digital rhetoricians is to work with components and processes at significantly smaller (and larger) scales. The ADXL 335 is a case in point. This device is a highly sophisticated machine, but its micro scale is well below the thresholds at which rhetoricians have worked traditionally. Learning how to botanize the materialities of this new era will require scaling down (or up) to levels in which the humanities have rarely had to work.

  Accelerometers detect changes in static and dynamic gravitational pull. Static or passive gravity is the earth's gravitational pull on one or more of the 335's three sensors. Dynamic gravity is the g-force of acceleration on

Transduction and Allegorized Style

one or more sensory axes. Conventional applications for an accelerometer include detecting vibration, tilt, and rapid acceleration and deceleration. A few examples include shutting down a washing machine when an excess of vibration indicates an unbalanced load, rotating the screen on a smartphone based on static gravitational changes to the X or Y axes, and deploying an air bag when a car comes to an abrupt stop, which is indicative of a crash.

Beyond the conventional "truths" for which sensors such as this one are designed is a wide range of transductive possibilities. From an inventional standpoint, once we know what the ADXL335 can sense, and the ranges, resolutions, and types of data that it transmits, a rhetor can practice a transductive science of the concrete in order to discover the available means of allegorization and eversion.

Discovering the Available Means of Transduction: A Multi-Stage, Recursive Process of Invention

The following annotated outline describes a seven-stage, recursive, inventional process for digital rhetors who are exploring the suasive possibilities of the era of physical computing. The goal of the inventional process that I developed is to work toward the discovery of the available means of transduction, and then to identify the ways in which a transductive process can be used to allegorize and then evert the reality associated with an audience's engagement with a physical computing object or event space. Each stage in the process begins with an italicized summary that offers an overview of the specific goal at hand and the kinds of questions a rhetor might need to answer. That summary is followed by an in-depth, technical explanation that serves to illustrate how the process works. While my focus on this specific sensor offers an explicit illustration of the process, the inventional process will change with each new sensor or actuator that a rhetor chooses to use. Chapters 2.5–5.5 demonstrate some of the variability that the inventional process goes through.

1. Learn about the technical characteristics and history of the component

Research the technical specs and history of the component. Exactly how does the component work? Is the component's ability to sense or act based on a chemical or physical change? What is the history behind the use of that chemical or physical process? This "low-level" investigation can also include research about the company that manufactures the component, its ecological footprint, a literature review of projects that have used it, a comparative study of related components in the marketplace, and a study of the component's cost-effectiveness or fit.

The way in which a MEMS accelerometer senses changes in motion is simple, elegant, and creative. Figure 17 below shows an illustration of the electro-mechanics on which it is based. Beginning with the mechanics, an "H-shaped" structure with a series of "tongues" is designed to respond to changes in static or dynamic gravitational force. As the "intertial mass" sways back and forth with changes in gravitation, the tongues move toward one or the other wall of two stationary fingers. The tongues and stationary fingers define what is known as a differential capacitor, which is the transductive basis for identifying a change in gravity.

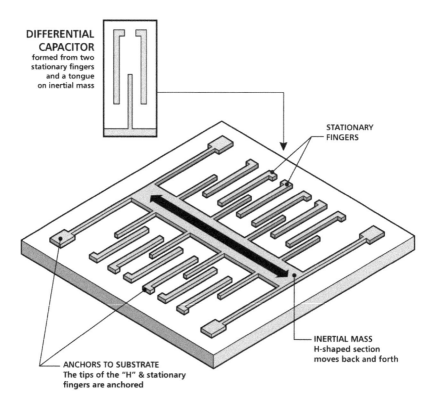

Figure 17. Diagram of H-Shaped MEMS Accelerometer. Photo credit: Bill Hammack.

An appreciation for the basic, technical characteristics of a differential capacitor leads us to a discussion of the electrical characteristics of this sensory machine. The characteristics are fascinating because they demonstrate how creative the computational foundations of this and many other sensory objects are. To understand what is involved requires an un-

Transduction and Allegorized Style

derstanding of capacitance, capacitors, and the ways in which measurable changes in the flow of electricity are used creatively as the basis of measuring movement.

For our purposes, capacitance will be a relatively simple concept. It is defined as the ability of a body to store an electrical charge. One of the conventional devices for storing an electrical charge is a parallel plate capacitor, which is an electrical circuit that has two conductive plates or surfaces separated by a dielectric. A dielectric is a non-conductive insulator that acts both as a barrier between the two conductive surfaces and as a space in which an electrostatic charge can be built up and stored. Dielectric materials are wide ranging and include solids, gases, and liquids. Porcelain, many plastics, air, nitrogen, mineral oil, and purified water are all dielectrics.

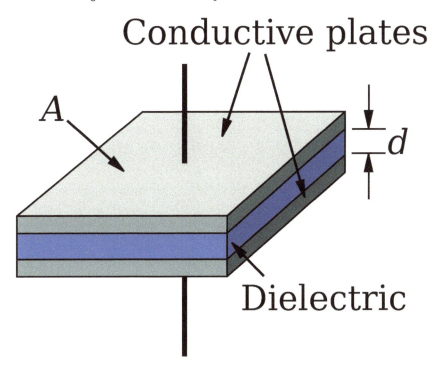

Figure 18. Illustration of a parallel-plate capacitor. Photo credit: Wikimeia Commons.

When an electrical charge is not able to flow from one conductive surface to the other, electrons build up, generating a potential difference between the two surfaces. That potential difference is the capacitance of the body. Before we turn to the electro-mechanics of the "differential capacitor," there is one more point that needs to be mentioned. In a parallel-plate

capacitor, capacitance is directly proportional to the size of the two conductive surfaces and inversely proportional to the distance or thickness of
the dielectric insulator. All things being equal, we can define capacitance
by measuring the areas of the two conductive surfaces and the thickness or
depth of the dielectric. Capacitance is a geometrical expression. Rhetorically, we might equate it with parallel schemes such as *antimetabole* or *chiasmus*.

Returning to Figure 17, in a differential capacitor, the dielectric is
air, and the "tongue" in between the two stationary "fingers" separates the
dielectric space into two halves. When the tongue moves back and forth,
the physical dimensions of the two dielectrical spaces separating the fingers
from each other are changed, which changes the electrical charge in the differential capacitor. Those differential changes in the dielectric space, which
allow electricity to flow, are then measured. The measurable differences in
electrical flow represent changes in motion. The measurable differences
from each of the three sensors are then converted from analog to digital
data, processed, and sent as numerical data to any number of devices. The
device can use the data to trigger one or more actuators, or it can be sent out
from the device to software programs running nearby or in the cloud. All of
this occurs dozens of times each second.

2. Identify the digital/numerical range(s) of data with which you will
be working

*Develop a simple software program and electrical circuit for your component, so you can determine
the high and low ranges of digital/numerical values with which you'll be working. This range will be
the basis for transduction in step 4. If you are working with an actuator, determine the kinds of data
with which your components work, and then write values to the component, to see how it works. If
you are working with a sensor, use the software program to read the values from the component, so
you know the actual range with which you will be working. If you are working with Arduino, you
will read or send values to/from your component in the Serial Monitor.*

Identifying the analog and digital ranges of a component is the basis
for allegorization because they define the ranges on which transduction is
based. These ranges are building blocks for the suasive goal of eversion.

Beginning with the analog voltage ranges, the data sheet for the
ADXL 335 stipulates a range of 1.8-3.6 volts. That means that we can use
any voltage within that range. The Arduino UNO has two voltages with
which to work, 5 and 3.3 volts; so, we will use 3.3 volts. The analog values
are on a continuum. They can be any number of values between 0-3.3 volts,
such as 0.025, 1.78, and 3.29. Digital values, on the other hand, are either
on or off, 1 or 0, high or low, which means that we need a way to divide the
continuum into two values—and more if we want higher resolution of our
analog data.

Transduction and Allegorized Style

In a video titled "Analog to Digital Signals," Jeremy Blum asks how we can convert the continuous, analog flow of electricity into a discrete, digital form of energy based on 1s and 0s. The solution is a device known as an analog-to-digital converter (ADC). Blum offers a general overview of the ways in which ADCs work. The first characteristic that he describes is their resolution, which is the number of bits into which the converter divides the analog continuum. The Arduino UNO has a 10-bit converter, which is resolution of 2^{10}. That 10-bit converter will offer 1024 points of resolution, or 0-1023. Blum explains that the analog signal is then divided among 10 logic levels. The 5 volts that the Arduino offers is divided evenly from 0 to the 5-volt threshold. Blum concludes, "Once we have a number, we can do whatever we want with it."

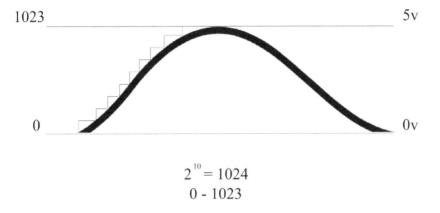

Figure 19. Representation of a 2^{10} converter. Video credit: Jeremy Blum.

The 0-1023 range is for the 5-volt analog signal. Since our threshold is 3.3, our digital range will stop at 675. That means that as we move forward with our project, we will be working with an analog voltage range of 0-3.3, which, divided among the 676 digital values, means that the resolution of the analog range is 0.0048~ volts.

Each sensor uses the analog/voltage range differently, so the range is little more than a stepping stone to the real values with which we'll work. In order to identify the ways in which the sensor's measurements can be "enhanced, embellished, and transposed," it is necessary to take a closer look at exactly what the ADXL 335 measures. Analog Devices' data sheet for the device lists the following:

> The product measures acceleration with a minimum full-scale range of +- 3 g. It can measure the static acceleration of gravity in tilt-sens-

Suasive Iterations

ing applications as well as dynamic acceleration resulting from motion, shock, or vibration. (1)

Static acceleration of gravity means that when the sensor is tilted, the force of gravity on one or more axes of the sensor will be registered. This measurement can be used to define angle or tilt. Dynamic acceleration is g-force. The measurements related to it can be used to describe vibration and other kinds of movement. In sum, the accelerometer will measure direction or tilt, movement, and the gravitation force of that movement.

The next step is to define the range of values with which we have to work. In theory, we are working with 0-675 digital values, but for a variety of reasons, the specific ranges will vary. The ADXL 335 senses changes in two kinds of gravity, static and dynamic. When the ADXL 335 is placed on a flat surface, it maintains a voltage that is supposed to be in the middle of its range, which is 1.65 volts, or an approximate digital value in the 330s. When it is tilted along one or more of its axes, the values change linearly. Figure 20 shows a read-out of the ranges that the sensor measures for tilt/direction.

These numbers are the basis for transduction and allegorization. As you write them down, identifying the lower, middle, and high value points for each axis, you'll notice that the values across the axes are not exactly the same. This is not uncommon. It is one of the reasons for taking the time to chart the analog ranges at the beginning of a project as well as recursively, when some of the parameters of a project has changed.

Transduction and Allegorized Style

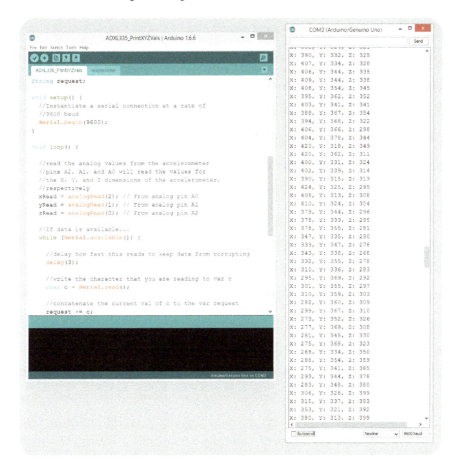

Figure 20. Screenshot of Arduino IDE (left) and Serial Monitor (right)

3. Develop a list of the ambient or direct, user-initiated actions your component can sense, or the kinds of actions your actuator can perform

List as many ways in which the component could be used to sense or act on the world. If your component is a sensor, make a list of the various kinds of sensory activities and changes that it can read. You shoud include sensory activities that go beyond the most obvious. For example, if you are working with a light-dependent resistor (LDR), in addition to listing 'changes in natural and artificial light levels,' you can list related causes for changes in those levels, such as pedestrians passing in front of a lit window, a cloudy sky, or, if the sensor is embedded in an object with a door or lid, actions related to opening and closing the object. If your component is an actuator, make a list of the various actions it can perform. As with the sensor, your list should include actions that go beyond the most obvious. For example, if you are working with a DC stepper motor, in addition to listing 'axle turns incrementally clockwise,' you can list related effects, such as 'turns the minute hand in a homemade analog clock,' or 'raises and lowers the string to which an object is attached.'

We are now ready to develop a list of events, actions, and ambient changes for which the component is designed. The following list is divided between static and dynamic types. For the static list, a starting or base position is assumed:

Static acceleration:

Right-side up

Upside down

Tilted or rotated away from base

Motionless

Dynamic acceleration:

Swinging/swaying

Shaking/shivering

Vibrating/trembling

Shocked (hit)

Slammed

Thrown

Identifying the range of states and actions that a sensor can detect is an essential step in the inventional process associated with allegorization, because these are the kinds of states and actions that will be represented by the data ranges charted in stage 2; as such, they are the states and actions on which transduction will be based.

4. Identifying the Ways in which to Allegorize the Data

Based on the list from stage 3, develop a list of the ways in which you can allegorize the data toward one or more suasive ends. Think about the ways in which events, actions, and other types of change listed in stage 3 can be associated with more specific natural or socio-cultural events. For example, dynamic acceleration associated with a swinging/swaying motion could be associated with the swing of a baseball bat, the swaying motion of a tree branch, or the movement of a swing in a playground.

After stage 3, the next inventional step is to associate one or more of the events, actions, and ambient changes from your list with a specific context in which those states and/or actions will become meaningful in a suasive context. A list of the ways in which to allegorize items from your list in stage 3 could include the following:

Transduction and Allegorized Style

Allegorize the moment of judgment in a judicial proceeding: the sensor is placed under the striking plate for a gavel, and the shock of the hit is measured and recorded

Allegorize the Great American Pastime: the sensor is placed in a baseball bat, and the dynamic acceleration of a swing is measured and recorded

Allegorize the sport of cycling: the sensor is attached to bicycle spokes and the rotation, dynamic acceleration, and shocks/bumps are recorded

Allegorize a person's gestures: the sensor is placed in a glove or other piece of clothing in order to record the wearer's movements

Allegorize a user's handling of an object: the sensor is embedded within an object, and the user's handling is tracked

Allegorize a natural flow, such as the wind or moving water: the sensor is placed in a kite or a boat, and the object's movements are recorded

The ability to allegorize one of the states or actions listed in stage 3 is based on a transduction of the data identified in stage 2. Stages 2-4 are essential to the process of developing a suasive, everting project.

5. Develop a "visualization dashboard" of the data

Develop a software program that I call a "visualization dashboard." The visualization is a useful way to think through the uses of the data—how to transduce them in any number of ways—especially when you are working collaboratively. The reason is that the visualization makes it easier to explain how otherwise abstract numerical thresholds might be conceptualized toward an everted end; moreover, it is easier to recognize how changes in the transduction of one or more values contribute to new possibilities for allegorization and eversion. While the visualization dashboard is not designed for an end-user—its purpose is to serve the inventional process—some of the code that is written for it will be reused. The dashboard helps you and your team figure out how to accomplish some of your suasive goals in code.

The penultimate inventional step is to develop a visualization dashboard of the data on which allegorization will be based. The dashboard is an important way in which to fully explore the available means of transduction by visualizing the effects of transductions that you perform on the data. In Figure 21 below, the three dimensions of sensory data are presented as three separate lines that grow from left to right across the screen. The numerical data is presented along the right-hand side of the screen, streaming vertically. In the graph, the three dimensions are colorized. The most recent 18 seconds of data are visualized on the screen.

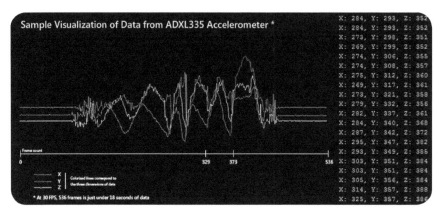

Figure 21. Sample visualization of data from an ADXL335 accelerometer.

As you play with the ADXL 335 accelerometer—turning it upside down or tilting it (static gravity), shaking or swinging it (dynamic gravity)—the visualization will help you identify moments of convergence when lines associated with two or all three of the dimensions of data cross over each other. Those moments of convergence can be a novel way in which to define a point at which a transduction of the data can be allegorized. This stage can be added to stages 2-4 as essential to the process of developing a suasive, everting project.

6. From visualization dashboard to allegorizing/everting software program(s)

Based in part on the code for your visualization dashboard, develop a "first draft" of the software that will serve the everting, suasive end of your project.

This final stage moves beyond invention because it involves the development of the software program that will transduce and allegorize the sensory data from the sensor toward an everting, suasive end. At this point, your software program will need to be associated with an inventional process that extends to the actuators that will be an important part of the process of eversion. Sound, image, text, and kinetic forms of movement and animation will be controlled by the software program that you write, which in turn will be based on the transductions and allegorizations that you've identified in stages 2-5. An early prototype of a project based on the ADXL 335 accelerometer is described in Chapter 2.5.

7. Refine the software program through a recursive process of re-invention

When a physical computing project is redesigned in some way—when changes have been made to the angle or position of one or more components, the ambient characteristics of the space in which the project is installed, or the rhetorical constraints of the audience—you may need to revise the data ranges for one or more sensors or actuators. When this happens, you will need to return to stage 2 or to stage 4, and then work your way back through to stage 6.

Small, almost imperceptible, changes can alter the data ranges on which your code is based, or some of the transductive actions, events, or ambient changes on which the project relies. For example, after installing a project based on the ADXL 335 accelerometer, you may realize that vibrations from user-related movements near the work are adding data spikes to one or more axes of the three-dimensional sensor. It could be vibrations attributed to heavy footsteps or to hands on a table or wall that is contiguous to the component.

Eversion from Allegorization

Based on the stylistic allegorization of transduced analog data from the ADXL335 sensor, eversion can serve as a new form of rhetorical appeal. Eversion, or the folding of some of the affordances of the virtual into the real, is an opportunity to transform a participant's conventional relationship with an action, position, or general experience with an interactive object or event space. That process implies one or more feedback loops. In *How We Became Posthuman*, N. Katherine Hayles writes the following in relation to feedback loops: "the idea of the feedback loop implies that the boundaries of the autonomous subject are up for grabs, since feedback loops can flow not only within the subject but also between the subject and the environment" (2). In simple terms, a feedback loop is a system in which inputs are transduced and returned as outputs contributing to a potentially endless causal chain of reactions. When we replace the traditional, liberal humanist subject with one who is embodied, and whose experience of self is based on a series of stable feedback loops, eversion takes on a new level of rhetorical importance. When a rhetor feeds back into an event-space the transduced and allegorized data associated with a participant's position or actions, she engages in an artful deviation of the energy associated with one or more implicit feedback loops comprising the participant's conventional sense of things. To evert is to alter the reality that is expressive of one or more feedback loops constitutive of an embodied experience. In a casuistically stretched, neo-Bitzerian sense, this is a rhetorical act of suasion, a mode of appeal supporting an explicit or implicit rhetorical claim. Learning how to botanize a sensor like the ADXL 335 is a step toward a new and compelling way in which to transduce the energy associated with a feedback loop. When you change the conventional way in which that energy is experienced, you have everted their experience toward suasive ends.

2.5 Writing with Three-Dimensional Wa(y)ves

Yes, "writing" is about sea CHANGE. And that, my d.ear.est, is why we are afraid of the thing called W~R~I~T~I~N~G~, and why we insist on "teaching" writing and IN institutions! I understand that YOU are afraid of the DRUNKEN BOAT.

—Victor Vitanza, "Abandoned to Writing"

Three origami paper boats, ADXL 335 accelerometers, and XBee radio transmitters. A partial tech list for a networked, wireless armada—a project inspired by two sources. The first is a poignant scene of loss, hope, and remembrance in the The Chinese Room's first-person game, *Dear Esther*.

Figure 22. Screen capture of origami boats in *Dear Esther*. Photo credit: The Chinese Room.

Dear Esther was first developed by Dan Pinchbeck as a mod using the Source game engine; so, the story is experienced from a first-person point of view. It takes place on a deserted island in the Scottish Hebrides. The unidentified, shipwrecked protagonist is injured and somewhat delusional. He is still mourning the death of his wife, Esther, who was killed in a car wreck on the mainland sometime in the past. As we make our way across the island toward a red, blinking beacon in the distance, the protagonist recites snippets of the letters he has written to his deceased wife—letters that he'll eventually fold into an armada of paper boats and send off to sea.

Suasive Iterations

A theme of writing is developed throughout the story that resonates with the approach to writing in this book. Graffiti writing, abstruse equations, and circuit drawings are found on cave walls and large rock faces across the island. In response to them, the protagonist explains, "We will scrawl in dead languages and electrical diagrams and hide them away for future theologians to muse and mumble over" (*Dear Esther*).

Figure 22 above is a screen shot of the candlelit cove where the protagonist's boats are floating. When we enter the cove, the protagonist describe the scene as follows:

> From here I can see my armada. I collected all the letters I'd ever meant to send to you, if I'd have ever made it to the mainland but had instead collected at the bottom of my rucksack, and I spread them out along the lost beach. Then I took each and every one and I folded them into boats. I folded you into the creases and then, as the sun was setting, I set the fleet to sail. (*Dear Esther*)

It is a poignant and provocative description of loss and hope as well as of writing.

The second source is also about loss, hope, and remembrance. Since 2015, hundreds of migrants and refugees fleeing countries in Africa and the Middle East have drowned in the Mediterranean Sea. Filled beyond capacity, scores of boats have capsized or sunk on their way to islands off the coasts of Greece and Italy. One of many images associated with the tragedy is the drowning of Alan Kurdi, a 3-year old Syrian boy fleeing his war-torn country with his family. The three-year old boy was among sixteen passengers in a rubber inflatable boat designed for eight that capsized soon after embarking for the Greek island of Kos. A picture of his lifeless body washed up on a beach went viral, prompting a response from governments internationally.

Inspired by *Dear Esther*'s armada of paper boats, and especially by the tragic drownings of hundreds of refugees and migrants in the Mediterranean, the goal is to promote awareness of the plight of migrants and refugees crossing the Mediterranean for Europe; so, the argumentative claim will be associated with the qualitative stasis (this issue is exigent; you must do something about it). A physical computing project comprising a series of paper origami boats will be the basis for the supporting argument that appeals to both pathos and logos. The boats can be relatively large (2-3 feet in length), and they can be crafted to be picked up and handled by participants in a gallery setting, or to float in a body of water. Based on sensory data from the ADXL 335 accelerometer, the analog data representative of the boats' movements can be the transductive basis for allegorization and eversion.

Writing with Three-Dimensional Wa(y)ves

Two ways in which to develop the physical computing project are as follows:

1. *Allegorizing participatory engagements with the boats.* A series of paper origami boats are placed in a gallery space. Each boat is associated with a specific capsizing. Written on it are the names of its passengers, survivors and victims. As participants pick up and handle the boats, they are implicated in an implicit, supporting argument that the lives of migrants and refugees are in their hands, too. The analog data associated with the participants' engagements with the boats can be the interface for an interactive, multimedia exhibit about the crisis in the Mediteranean. As one or more boats are picked up and handled, images, text, and sound associated with the boats and the crisis are enacted in the gallery.

2. *Allegorizing the motion of the boats floating in a body of water.* The body of water could be well known, with an important and symbolic history; in fact, it could be the Mediterranean. The analog data from the accelerometers (the bobbing up and down, tipping, and angling of the boats) can be transmitted to a computer on the shore or boat, which then transmits it wirelessly to another computer running the same interactive, multimedia project described above. Compared to the first project, which involves direct, participatory engagement, this particular project could be more contemplative; it favors a more logos-oriented appeal, compared to the pathetic appeal associated with having one of the boats (and its list of passengers) in your hands.

With these two approaches in mind, Figure 23 shows two diagrams depicting the technologies and networked connections that would be required.

In the first diagram on the left (1), which corresponds with project #1 described above, the three origami boats (A1) are located in the event space. Hidden in each of their triangular wheelhouses are a battery-powered Arduino microcontroller outfitted with an XBee radio module and an ADXL 335 accelerometer (see Figure 24).

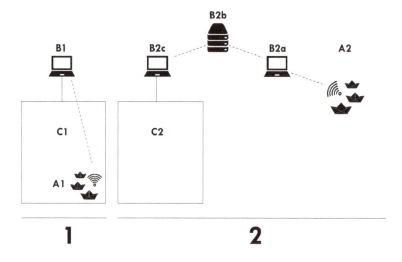

Figure 23. Diagrams of physical computing infrastructure.

Figure 24. 9-volt battery-powered Arduino with XBee shield and ADXL 335 accelerometer.

Writing with Three-Dimensional Wa(y)ves

The Arduino is continuously reading the three dimensions (X, Y, and Z) of accelerometer data from the sensor. Meanwhile, a PC located within a hundred feet of the boats (B1) is running a Processing sketch, which is in wireless communication with the Arduinos. The Processing sketch requests the accelerometer data from each of the Arduinos, transduces it, and then communicates changes to the various actuators (speakers, lights, screens, projectors, and so on) that are in the event space (C1). When participants in the event space pick up one or more of the boats, the ways in which they handle them are transduced toward stylistically allegorized ends and fed back into the space. Changes to the sounds, lighting, and projected images and text in the space are expressive of an allegorized handling of the boats leading to a potentially everted experience.

In the second diagram (2), which corresponds with project #2 described above, three origami boats are located outside the event space (A2). Let us imagine that they are floating within 100 feet of a PC on the shore (B2a). The boats are set up in the same way as above. The difference is that the Processing sketch to which the accelerometer data is being sent is written wirelessly to a database on a web-accessible server (B2b), which, in turn, is being read wirelessly by another Processing sketch running on a second PC (B2c). When the second PC reads new accelerometer data from the database, it transduces the nine dimensions of data from the three accelerometers (three, 3-dimensional accelerometers offer a rhetor nine data streams for transduction), allegorizing it toward an everted and suasive end in the event space in which participants are located.

Once an approach has been chosen and the basic hardware and software environment developed for it, you and your team would develop a simple software program. The program is part of step 2 in the inventional process outlined at the end of Chapter 2. It would help you identify the data ranges for all of the dimensions of accelerometer data. The ranges will be markedly different, depending on whether the boats are handled by participants in a gallery or floating freely in a body of water. Once you've identified the data ranges with which you'll be working, you can develop a list of events, actions, and ambient changes for which the component is designed; this is stage three. The list might include the following:

Pitching or rocking, fore, aft

Heaving, up, down

Rolling, starboard, aft

Yawing, back, forth

Capsized or beams up

Grounded (on shore)

Becalmed (motionless; safe)

The fourth step may be the most challenging one with this particular project. How do you want to allegorize the moment when a participant handling a boat turns it over, "capsizing" it? How do you want to allegorize the movements of boat floating in the water when a wave pitches it fore and aft? Answers to those questions will have a direct bearing on the way in which the interactive, multimedia project in the gallery is played.

A Visualization Dashboard for Transductive, Rhetorical Invention

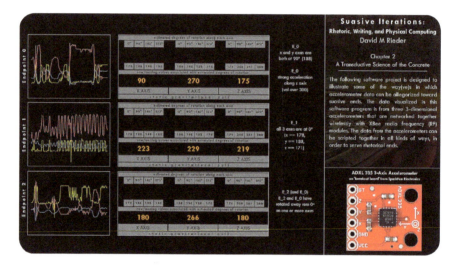

Figure 25. Visualization dashboard for ADXL 335 data streams.

With this particular project, it may be more productive to develop the visualization dashboard (stage 5) while you are brainstorming the ways in which to allegorize the transduced data. The reason is related to the number of data points with which you are working: if allegorization is based on the network of data points, the visualization will make it easier to conceptualize the most important points of connection among the boats. Figure 25 is a visualization dashboard that I developed for the data streaming from three boats. The visualizations in the left-hand column make it easier to recognize the rhythm and intensity of change—the flat-lines, spikes, and types of changes—across the nine data points. That visualization will help me get a "feel" for the data. The series of angular data points in the right-hand column are related to an approach that I wanted to explore, which was to

Writing with Three-Dimensional Wa(y)ves

look for moments when one or more dimensions of data across the three accelerometers crossed the same thresholds. Those crossings would be an opportunity to allegorize the data toward specific ends in the gallery. They also represent a type of remembrance within my coding for the victims who tried to cross the "inland" or "middle sea."

Once a set of stylistic approaches to the data have been identified, code developed for the dashboard in stage 5 can be used along with new code to draft the final version of the software for the participants/audience in the gallery (stage 6). As the project is relocated and/or you realize that audience members are not handling the boats in a gallery as you and your team had anticipated, you may have to return to one of the earlier stages in the inventional process (stage 7).

3 Onto-Allegories for the 'Great Outdoors'

The most profound technologies are those that disappear. They weave themselves into the fabric of everyday life until they are indistinguishable from it.

—Mark Weiser, "The Computer for the Twenty-First Century"

In April 2013, Twitter UK announced the creation of #Flock. The project was designed by Berg, a small UK-based design firm that closed in the fall of 2014. On their website, #Flock is described as a project designed for a limited number of Twitter's clients, as an award for creativity.

> A unique and very limited edition cuckoo clock, #Flock was made in collaboration with Twitter. A set of four houses, three contain colourful birds which react to Twitter triggers, the fourth is a simple clock. A new follower, a retweet or an @message will trigger one of the birds to pop out of its house, each with a different movement. Optional birdsong can accompany each action, the volume controlled with a small dial. (Berg)

In Figure 26, the white knob on the side of the first house on the left is the volume dial. The green-painted bird that is popping out of the roof signals a new follower. In the third and fourth houses, the birds that pop out of the holes signify a retweet and @message, respectively. The second house is an analog clock.

Figure 26. #Flock by Berg. Video credit: Oran O'Reilly.

Onto-Allegories for the 'Great Outdoors'

#Flock is an Arduino-based project that communicates with a cloud-based web service (a software program) via Berg's now-defunct "Berg Cloud." Compared to the project in Chapter 2.5, the only sensor-based transducer #Flock makes use of is a rotary potentiometer (the volume dial). The other transducers are actuators, namely, stepper motors to move the birds, and the speaker. The actuators combine to generate an eversion of the conventional experience and expectations of 'clock time' by allegorizing the idiosyncratic time of three types of social media events associated with a Twitter feed (new followers, retweets, and @messages).

#Flock is a well-executed example of an *everyware*. It is compelling and worth emulating—but it is also a project of which digital rhetors should be somewhat wary. As I will explain shortly, the desire to create objects that are calm, cool, and inconspicuous can be based on an anti-rhetorical attitude, a potential expression of which is found in the epigraph above. For digital rhetors and writers, whose field emerged in opposition to current-traditional tenets of clarity and brevity in prose writing, the desire to create everywares sounds like a related disposition. As Richard Lanham once said about the ideal of clarity in writing, it assumes a passive engagement with reality: "To write is to *compose* a world as well as *view* one. Prose can never be purely transparent because there is no purely self-subsisting model out there to be transparent to" (Analyzing 3). Likewise, everywares can never truly disappear or weave themselves into our lives; rather, they contribute to its composition.

Inspired in part by Lanham's rebuttal against clarity and Ian Bogost's theory of ontography, the following chapter is a call to a different kind of everyware—one that doesn't reinforce the notion that reality is apprehended passively. I call my preferred form of everyware onto-allegorical, for reasons that will become apparent shortly. In the remainder of this chapter, I summarize the goals of calm computing and offer a critique inspired by Lanham's argument against the C-B-S theory of prose as well as his theory of attention. Following Lanham, I summarize and explore the role that Ian Bogost's theory of ontography can play in a rhetorical approach to ubiquitous computing (UC) that is not encalming. Finally, I return to #Flock, to offer a description of how it can be revised in onto-allegorical terms.

Everywares and the Rise of Ubiquitous Computing

In Chapter 2, I cited Adam Greenfield's neologism, *everyware*, and quoted from his description of the growing range of "smart" household objects participating in the Janusian moment associated with the rise of post-PC technologies. I explained that everywares are designed to be two-faced. On the one hand (or face), they serve us like a Nietzschean truth, by calmly supporting some of our most basic routines; on the other hand (the "about face"), they participate in a noisy, gregarious, and globally-networked "dance of information." The logic of everywares is that the more engaged they are with technical networks and processes far from our view, the more proportionally personal they can be. In other words, the less human they are, the more human they can seem.

Compared to the PC, which is designed to fully support the most important activities in our working lives, everywares are designed to support the appurtenant, seemingly mundane issues that we manage on our way to those activities. Greenfield writes, "[Everywares] aim to answer questions as humble and important, as 'Where did I leave my keys?' 'Will I be warm enough in this jacket?' and 'What's the best way to drive to work this morning?'" (34). He explains that these issues may seem fleeting, "somehow interstitial to the real business of a life," but the interstices are precisely where we spend the majority of our days (33).

Their "interstitial" role is an engineered response to the exigence of information overload. UC was developed to address that exigence. In the 1990s, Researcher Mark Weiser and his team at Xerox PARC argued that interface design during the PC Era had focused exclusively on "dramatic machines." During the era, the "highest ideal" was to "make a computer so exciting, so wonderful, so interesting, that we never want to be without it" (2). In published remarks and essays, Weiser would later elaborate, explaining that the problem with this ideal is that a growing number of computers are now competing for our full attention. If the quantity of computers is increasing and our attention is limited, users will be overwhelmed. Weiser and his colleagues concluded that the UC era should be defined by computers that are less dramatic and attention-grabbing. The new ideal for the post-PC era is to develop "encalming" technologies.

In their essay "The Coming Age of Calm Technology," Weiser and John Seely Brown advocate the development of "calm technologies," characterized by their ability to shift dynamically from the center to the periphery of our attention as needed:

> Information technology is more often the enemy of calm. Pagers, cellphones, news services, the World-Wide-Web, email, TV, and radio bombard us frenetically. . . . But some technology does lead to true calm and comfort. There is no less technology involved in a comfortable pair of shoes, in a fine writing pen, or in delivering the New York Times on a Sunday morning, than in a home PC. Why is one often enraging, the others frequently encalming? We believe the difference is in how they engage our attention. Calm technology engages

both the *center* and the *periphery* of our attention, and in fact moves back and forth between the two. (1)

Examples of the ideal of calm abound in today's emerging post-PC era. Smartphones are a provocative example. Many of the apps running on them operate silently in the background until our attention is needed.

The call for calm, invisible technologies may seem to be an innovative response to the exigence of information overload, but rhetoricians and writing theorists may recognize them as an echo of the historical distrust of rhetoric. The following two quotations represent the call for what might be called "calm writing." The first is from Samuel Taylor Coleridge:

> The words in prose ought to express the intended meaning, and no more; if they attract attention to themselves, it is, in general, a fault. In the very best styles, such as Southey's, you read page after page, understanding the author perfectly, without once taking notice of the medium of communication. (110)

The second quotation is from Adams Sherman Hill's textbook, *Principles of Rhetoric*. It is from a section subtitled "Clearness" in which Hill's argument against attention-getting writing (and speaking) resembles Weiser's critique of the "dramatic machines" of the PC Era:

> [A writer or speaker] should remember that, so far as the attention is called to the medium of communication, so far is it withdrawn from the ideas communicated, and this even when the medium is free of flaws. How much more serious the evil when the medium obscures or distorts an object. (Hill 65)

If expressivist and cognitivist writing pedagogies circa the 1970s taught us anything, it is that the communicational ideals of invisibility (and calmness) espoused by Weiser and his colleagues are both nothing new and something of which to be wary. Calls for invisible and transparent computing echo the anti-rhetorical ideals of clarity and brevity against which scholars and practitioners of rhetoric and composition have long struggled. Richard Lanham offers some historical context for this point when he writes against the Clarity, Brevity-Sincerity (C-B-S) theory of prose. In the following quote from *Analyzing Prose* he emphasizes the anti-rhetorical drive behind C-B-S:

> The C-B-S theory argues that prose ought to be maximally transparent and minimally self-conscious, never seen and never noticed. . . . 'Rhetoric' in such a view very naturally becomes a dirty word, point-

ing to superficial ornament on the one hand and moral duplicity on the other. It becomes, that is, everything which interferes with the natural and efficient communication of ideas. 'Rhetoric' is what we should get rid of in prose. (1-2)

When Weiser claims that the "most profound technologies are those that disappear" (66), he is espousing the UC version of the C-B-S theory.

Another significant problem with Weiser's theory of UC is that it doesn't adequately foreground the following paradox: in order for UC technologies to serve us peripherally, they must exceed our grasp. They may appear to serve us, and do so with an even more personal touch than the desktop and laptop computers that preceded them, but their power to serve us is predicated on a computational dynamic to which we have only indirect access. The truth of these technologies is that their power resides in a global network of computational processes that they occlude from our view. For digital rhetoricians, an opportunity presents itself to evert some of that relationship between the personal and impersonal, which can be valued as an opportunity to overturn the faceless currency of truth established by calm technologies, generating subtle but suasive ripples of engagement and appeal in its place.

Disturbing the Distributed Peace

In "The Coming Age of Calm Technology," Mark Weiser and John Seely Brown explain how what Greenfield called everywares herald a "third phase" in popular computing. Writing twenty years ago, they postulated that the new era of computing would achieve crossover with the PC age between 2005 and 2020. The support for their argument is based on a comparative, three-phase history of computing that culminates in an age of UC.

The first two phases are the "Mainframe Era" and the "PC Era." The characteristic that determines the differences among the three eras is the user's relationship with the technology. Introducing the first phase, Weiser and Brown write, "Anytime a computer is a scarce resource, and must be negotiated and shared with others, our relationship is that of the mainframe era" (1). Compared to the first phase, the PC era is a one-to-one relationship: "You have your computer, it contains your stuff, and you interact directly and deeply with it" (1). Weiser and Brown add that any computer with which you have a personal relationship contributes to this era, which means that laptops, smartphones, and tablets are PCs, too.

Compared to the first and second eras, the UC era is defined by an inverted ratio between users and computers. Weiser and Brown introduce the comparative difference of UC as follows:

Onto-Allegories for the 'Great Outdoors'

> The "UC" era will have lots of computers sharing each of us. Some of these computers will be the hundreds we may access in the course of a few minutes of Internet browsing. Others will be embedded in walls, chairs, clothing, light switches, cars—in everything. UC is fundamentally characterized by the connection of things in the world with computation. (2)

In terms of the attention we pay to UC technologies, it would appear that humans now occupy the role that mainframe computers once played. Early mainframe computers addressed the issue of attention by defining how much and with whom process cycles would be shared. In a UC era, our attention is the "scarce resource," and UC machines must negotiate and share it with each other in order to gain our attention. A key point in Weiser and Brown's characterization of UC is at the end of this quote: UC is defined by the ability for all kinds of microtechnologies to engage with computational processes in a distributed, networked environment, an engagement that was made possible by internet and wireless communication protocols.

Such protocols have made it possible to connect all kinds of PCs, including household appliances, to broader processes of computation, which transforms those individualized technologies into nodes along an increasingly distributed network of engagement. They also invert the implicit ratio sustained during the first and second phases, during which one or more users poured their attention into one computer. In the UC era, the center of our attention is a constantly changing point of reference in relation to a distributed, computational field comprising numerous other processes—a never-ending series of micro-events.

Turning to their theory of "calm computing," Weiser and Brown charge, "If computers are everywhere they better stay out of the way, and that means designing them so that the people being shared by the computers remain serene and in control" (3). Due to the inverted ratio of users to computers, a more nuanced and dynamic way of engaging a user's attention has to be developed. Their solution is to develop a system in which a user's central focus can be shifted around as peripheral events require more attention: "Calm technology engages both the center and the periphery of our attention, and in fact moves back and forth between the two" (3). Human experience is a complex, overlapping range of phenomena eliciting our attention. The vast majority of the phenomena with which we are engaged are peripherally located, which is where "we are attuned but not attending to explicitly" (4). Only when a peripheral concern demands more of our attention do we shift our focus. It is the empowerment introduced by this dynamic that reduces the experience of information overload, "encalming" us. They conclude their essay with the following charge: "We must learn to design for the periphery so that we can most fully command technology without being dominated by it" (4).

The legacy of Weiser's theory of calm persists. In addition to Greenfield's book, there are works such as Paul Dourish and Genevieve Bell's *Diving the Digital Future: Mess and Mythology in Ubiquitous Computing*, which offers a detailed explanation of the legacy of Weiser's ideas in current trends, and several chapters in Ulrik Ekman's collection, *Throughout: Art and Culture Emerging with Ubiquitous Computing*. Based on these recent contributions, it is apparent that calm computing is a conceptual touchstone for UC and its offshoots pervasive computing, NUI, and what is known as the "Internet of Everything."

If the conservatism of Weiser's position isn't obvious to digital rhetoricians and writers, Weiser's theory of writing will help elucidate its limitations. In "The Computer for the 21st Century," Weiser describes writing as "perhaps the first information technology," but he then defines writing as "the ability to represent spoken language symbolically" (66). This view of writing is expressive of the conventional, logocentric definition against which writers, writing theorists, and artists have countered, in theory and practice, for over a century. Considering Weiser's interests in experimentation, it is unfortunate that his view of writing is so conventional and constrained. Over the past century, post-alphabetic approaches to and theories of writing abound, from Stéphane Mallarmé's turn-of-the-last-century experimentations with space and typography in *Un Coup de Dés*, the mid-twentieth-century experiments of the Oulipo and hypertextual, cybertextual, and technotextual literature and poetry in the late-twentieth, to more recent work associated with composition studies by Anne Wysocki, Gregory Ulmer, Craig Saper, Sarah Arroyo, Jody Shipka, Madeleine Sorapure, and many others.

Weiser's logocentric assumptions about writing are telling because they are symptomatic of an instrumentalist approach to technology in his approach to UC. In other words, he values computer technologies for their service role, not as a generative medium of open-ended experimentation. As innovative as he was, his answer to the question of limited attention is conservative.

The parallels between Weiser's technological response to the excesses of attention-getting machines and a century of social theory about the impact of modern and postmodern techno-culture on humanity are worth noting. Since the turn of the last century, numerous critical theorists have argued vehemently against the rise of modern and postmodern communication technologies. From Georg Simmel's early-twentieth-century concerns about the blasé attitude in metropolitan (read: urban) cultures, Walter Benjamin's mid-twentieth-century concerns about the "fiery glow" of capitalist

Onto-Allegories for the 'Great Outdoors'

culture, Theodore Adorno and Max Horkheimer's critiques of the culture industry, Paul Virilio's near-paranoid late-twentieth-century concerns about real-time telecommunication technologies, to Frederic Jameson's despair over the excesses of postmodernity, there has been a continuous concern about the impact of our industrial and post-industrial techno-cultures on human thought and action. Weiser has come up with an innovative solution, but it is one that plays into the implicitly conservative view of humanity in the abovementioned critical theories.

In the early 1980s, Jean Baudrillard appeared to challenge the conservatism of critical theorists by embracing a "post-dialectical" view of change. The opening page of his book, *Fatal Strategies*, begins as follows: "Things have found a way of avoiding a dialectics of meaning that was beginning to bore them: by proliferating indefinitely, increasing their potential, outbidding themselves in an ascension to the limit, an obscenity that henceforth becomes their immanent finality and senseless reason" (7). Baudrillard is not celebrating the new reality, but neither is he willing to forgo its role in our techno-futures. Some critics have characterized his "fatal" approach as ironic, but taken at his word, he is calling for us to work *with* excess.

Baudrillard's position is a provocative one, in light of the paradox of everyware technologies. The "dance of information" about which Greenfield wrote is a post-dialectical dynamic, and Weiser's encalming solution, which upholds the centrality of the human in relation to the excesses of attention-getting computers, finds its success in technologies that are post-dialectical. The two-faced structure of everyware technologies—the dynamic that makes them encalming—is tilted toward the non-human.

For digital rhetoricians, Weiser's conservative approach to the excesses of our information age can be counter-productive. It attempts to suppress the noisy dance of information to which everywares are inextricably linked. An approach to everywares that foregrounds (read: allegorizes) some of that dance, and that does it with a more dynamic understanding of attention in its sights, has the potential to extend some of the avant-garde work that has been developed under the auspices of rhetoric and composition in the past twenty years.

Post-Correlationism, Attention Traps, and Ontographs

Borrowing a term from philosopher Quentin Meillassoux, UC technologies are "post-correlationist." Correlationism is Meillassoux's self-described philosopheme for the predominance of this philosophical approach since Immanuel Kant. In the following excerpt from his book, *After Finitude*, Meillassoux defines the term:

By "correlation" we mean the idea according to which we only ever have access to the correlation between thinking and being, and never to either term considered apart from the other. We will henceforth call *correlationism* any current of thought which maintains the unsurpassable character of the correlation so defined. . . . Correlationism consists in disqualifying the claim that it is possible to consider the realms of subjectivity and objectivity independently of one another. (5)

Since Immanuel Kant's correlationist turn to a transcendental subject to which being would be inextricably linked, modern philosophy has trapped being in a subjective realm. To understand both Meillassoux's definition and its association with Kantian thought, a brief review of David Hume's necessity argument is required. In his *Treatise of Human Nature*, Hume argues that it is not possible to identify necessary causal relations, if our knowledge of those relations is derived from our senses. One of the best known examples in support of his claim centers on two billiard balls. Hume argues that while he may believe that when one ball hits another it transfers its force, thus demonstrating cause and effect, he cannot find any observable proof of this belief. Cause and effect and other causal relations are thus beliefs without necessary proof. In his critique of Hume's skepticism, Kant argues that objects conform to the mind, not the other way around. Since the mind gives form and structure to objects, necessity does not need to be discovered in the sensory realm. Instead, it is given by the transcendental subject who organizes a priori its experiences of the world.

According to Meillassoux, Kant's argument establishes a correlation between thought and thing, subject and object, which would predominate philosophy and theory throughout the modern period. In his summary of Meillassoux's argument, Levi Bryant writes, "With the inauguration of [Kantian] correlationism we get a battle of the correlationists" (Bryant). Whether it is Husserl, Wittgenstein, Habermas, cultural Marxists, or the hermeneutists, correlationism is implied. Bryant writes, "All of these orientations agree in the basic claim that the object is only an object for a subject and the subject is only a subject for the object, and that we never know an object as it is in-itself independent of the structures that condition appearances" (Bryant).

The work of Meillassoux, Bryant, Graham Harman and several other philosophers has been linked to the movement, speculative realism. In *Alien Phenomenology*, Bogost writes of speculative realism that "The speculative realists share a common position less than they do a common enemy: the tradition of human access that seeps from the rot of Kant" (4). Bogost

Onto-Allegories for the 'Great Outdoors'

explains that for the speculative realists, the first step is to reject correlationism. In the following excerpt, Bogost elaborates on this step:

> To be a speculative realist, one must abandon the belief that human access sits at the center of being, organizing and regulating it like an ontological watchmaker. In both a figurative and literal sense, speculative realism is an *event* rather than a philosophical position. It names a moment when the epistemological tide ebbed, revealing the iridescent shells of realism they had so long occluded. (5)

Based on Bogost's argument, my claim is that Weiser's thesis of calm is correlationist. It re-introduces a Kantian high tide in which the "iridescent shells of realism" (and the faces of Nietzsche's coins) are covered over.

Considering the extent to which persuasion is a strategic pull toward change—a centrifugal post-correlationaist *wayve*—Weiser's "keep calm" approach can be characterized as anti-rhetorical, which is why finding ways in which to disturb the distributed peace is an important step forward. Two theorists who offer both rhetoricians and writers the basis for such a move are Richard Lanham and Ian Bogost. By combining Richard Lanham's rhetorical theory of attention and Bogost's post-correlationist theory of ontography, a digital rhetoric of onto-allegories can be proposed as an alternative to Weiser's legacy of calm.

Attention in a Weightless World

In *The Economics of Attention: Style and Substance in the Age of Information*, Richard Lanham begins by stating, "The age of information has brought with it a strange paradox. Just when we are drowning in stuff, we seem to be abolishing it" (1). Lanham is alluding to a well-documented trend toward the immaterialization of socio-economic value in the United States and other post-industrializing nations since the end of World War II. Alan Greenspan, who is credited with first characterizing the economy as increasingly "weightless," helped popularize an understanding of the trend in 1996. In the published remarks of his speech, he begins with the following historical description:

> The world of 1948 was vastly different from the world of 1996. The American economy, more then than now, was viewed as the ultimate in technology and productivity in virtually all fields of economic endeavor. The quintessential model of industrial might in those days was the array of vast, smoke-encased integrated steel mills in the Pittsburgh district and on the shores of Lake Michigan. Output was things, big physical things. (Greenspan)

Suasive Iterations

Greenspan continues, citing the dramatic shift from an economy based on "physical resources and human brown in the production of goods and services" to one in which concepts and ideas, designs, computer code, and other post-industrial offerings predominate. Greenspan cites numerous examples including the following one:

> Turn-of-the-century steel mills, and even those operating in 1948, valued the physical brawn that could move coiled sheets from one segment of a plant to another. Today, we perform these tasks with devices whose mechanical leverage is designed and guided by the insights coded into a computer program. (Greenspan)

Greenspan concludes, "Accordingly, while the weight of current economic output is probably only modestly higher than it was a half century ago, value added, adjusted for price change, has risen well over threefold" (Greenspan). His conclusion is the source of the credit he received for introducing the concept of weightlessness. Soon after its publication, several books in business and economic theory, including Diane Coyle's *The Weightless World* and Charles Leadbetter's *The Weightless Society*, would reference it.

For Lanham, the shift to an increasingly immaterial or weightless socio-economy—in other words, the shift to an age of information—introduces "a fundamental figure/ground reversal in how we think about the world we live in" (6). Traditionally, concepts and ideas are about the physical world, about Greenspan's "big physical things." But in an information age, this equation is reversed. Now, concepts and ideas are the generative basis of the physical world. The physical world is the derivative. The physical is an expression or manifestation of concepts and ideas.

There is a second figure/ground reversal that follows from the one described above: concepts and ideas, i.e., information, are not scarce. In fact, they are overly abundant. This second reversal is an issue because, classically, economics focuses on how human beings allocate scarce resources. If information is not scarce, Lanham asks, "What then is the new scarcity that economics seek to describe?" (*Economics* 7). Lanham's answer is that the new scarcity is attention: "It can only be the human attention needed to make sense of information" (8). As Lanham investigates what he calls the "attention economy," he underscores a key difference between attention and the kinds of physical objects and resources on which the preceding economy was based. The point he develops is that attention does not fit the mold of a traditional commodity. Lanham introduces the quandary as follows. He explains that in the preceding industrial economy, the one that produced "big physical things," the term capital was used to define "what is needed to capture, produce, and preserve goods" (4). But in today's post-industrial,

Onto-Allegories for the 'Great Outdoors'

weightless economy, attention does not fit this definition. Instead, it is a dynamic immaterial force. Thus, Lanham states, "It is more like a poetry reading than a profit-and-loss statement" (8). Moreover, attention tends to have a transformative affect on the objects with which it is engaged. Like a melody, it transforms the individual notes associated with it.

Lanham goes on to critique economist Herbert Simon's response to the question of attention. In the following quote, Lanham underscores how Simon's response implies a "'commodity' thinking" about attention:

> Herbert Simon considered the attention-economy problem in 1971 and saw it as simply a question of filtering. Computer "knowbots," as we now call them, digital librarians, would organize our attention for us; our news would arrive pre-Googled and personalized. Or we would hire live special librarians to step in where Google fails. . . . Either way, bots or bodies, the thinking remains "commodity" thinking. We have too many boxes of information arriving at our loading dock. We must find mechanized ways to organize their arrival. A UPS problem. (8)

Lanham counters, "Human attention is more complicated than that" (8). It is not a "thing" that can be filtered out.

After claiming that attention is not a commodity, and that his goal is to identify persuasive forms of attention-getting, Lanham asks: to whom we should turn for inspiration? To whom can we turn for ideas about developing compelling "attention structures"? His answer is the visual arts. Lanham explains his reasoning as follows: "In the twentieth century, the most obvious economists of attention have been the visual artists. The locus of art, for them, became not the physical object that occasioned the aesthetic response but the response itself. The center of art migrated from the object to the attention it required" (15). In a chapter titled "Economists of Attention," Lanham highlights the work of Andy Warhol. Supporting his claim that Warhol is engaging with economic issues, Lanham cites Warhol's own statements about the relationship between art and business:

> Business art is the step that comes after Art. I started as a commercial artist, and I want to finish as a business artist. . . . Being good in business is the most fascinating kind of art . . . making money is art and working is art and good business is the best art. (Warhol qtd. in Lanham 48)

According to Lanham, the best art in which Warhol engaged was attention-getting. His series of Campbell's soup cans are his case in point.

Suasive Iterations

Lanham explains how Warhol's exhibition at the Ferus Gallery in Los Angeles attracted a wide range of attention from the critics, curators, fellow artists; reactions from the public would arrive later. Early reactions from critics represented a frustration with what seemed utterly superficial and meaningless: "These soup cans had to mean *something*. . . . There had to be *some* soup in the can" (49). It is worth noting that reactions to Warhol's soup cans echo critiques of Random International's "Rain Room."

Lanham calls Warhol's soup cans an "attention trap." In the following excerpt, he expands on the ways in which these cans acted as a trap (i.e., a dynamic framework into which meaning was drawn).

> [Warhol's soup cans] created a powerful yet economical attention trap. A maximum of commentary was created by a minimum of effort. Subject? Off the shelf. Basic design? Off the shelf. Technique? Ditto. Replication? Silk screen, off the shelf, too. . . . Altogether, a dynamite niche product at a bargain basement cost. (50)

Warhol created a framework for a rhetorical event—and he did it with off-the-shelf materials. Like Duchamp's Readymades, Warhol demonstrated how maximum attentional profit could be generated with minimal input.

For digital rhetoricians, the ability to disturb the distributed peace begins with a more sophisticated understanding of attention. It begins with the recognition that attention is not a generic quantity (read: commodity). As we realize how attention works—how it is elicited—then we can work toward projects that create attention-getting traps based on eversions of the conventional line between the real and the virtual. These eversions have the potential to expose some of the irridescence of the post-correlationist dance of information that is otherwise occluded by the "truth" of calm.

Ontography and the "Great Outdoors"

In *Alien Phenomenology*, Ian Bogost develops a method for both discovering and mapping out some of the relational dimensions of a post-correlationist world, which he calls "ontography." For Bogost, ontography is an heuristic for experiencing what he calls, borrowing the phrase from Quentin Messailloux, the "great outdoors." Bogost explains that Meillassoux's phrase is meant "to describe the outside reality that correlationism had stolen from philosophy" (38). In the following excerpt, Bogost offers a compelling reason for the move beyond correlationism: "Once we put down the trappings of culture and take the invitation into that great outdoors, a tremendous wave of surprise and unexpectedness would overwhelm us—a 'global ether' of incredible novelty and unfamiliarity" (38). In order to reach this

Onto-Allegories for the 'Great Outdoors'

post-correlationist stance, Bogost introduces ontography as a "general in-scriptive strategy, one that uncovers the repleteness of units and their inter-objectivity" (38).

Bogost ties his interest in the anti-correlationism of speculative re-alism to his theory of "unit operations," which is the subject of his book, *Unit Operations*. In the first chapter of that book, Bogost presents a theoretical basis for the term that will ultimately serve the critical ends of his book; the subtitle of his book is "An Approach to Videogame Criticism."

Bogost claims that the "unit operation" is a new conceptual basis for studying the characteristics and elements of a wide range of source texts, including games. He writes, "Unit analysis is the name I suggest for the general practice of criticism through the discovery and exposition of unit operations at work in one or more source texts" (15). His chapter is divided in two parts. The first half is devoted to defining his terms, and the second half is about its analytical/critical possibilities. Since the second half does not serve the inventional ends that I'm exploring in this book, I'll focus on the first half.

Bogost begins *Unit Operations* by stating his interest in "unpacking" the relationships between criticism and computation. To this end, he of-fers an opposed pair of terms, unit- and system operations, defining the terms initially as follows: "Unit operations are modes of meaning-making that privilege discrete, disconnected actions over deterministic, progressive systems" (3). The "deterministic, progressive systems" is his allusion to sys-tems operations. Bogost also writes, "In general, unit operations privilege function over context, instances over longevity" (4).

Compared to unit operations, systems operations promote "stabil-ity, linearity, universalism, and permanence." They sacrifice openness for certainty. They are "characteristically protracted, dependent sequential, and static" (4). And they "imply a fundamental or universal order that an agent might 'discover'" (6). With these descriptions in mind, we can add that sys-tems operations presume a transcendental cause, origin, or end that defines and regulates the meaning and operations of the units within its limits.

To further define his terms, Bogost elaborates on the origins and meanings of three terms: unit, system, and operation. A unit is "a material element, a thing" (5). It can operate at different levels and scales: "It can be constitutive or contingent, like a building block that makes up a system, or it can be autonomous, like a system itself" (5). Bogost explains that his unit has a lot in common with philosopher Graham Harman's objects. In Harman's object-oriented philosophy, Bogost explains, "all objects in the world, not just humans, are fundamentally referential, or form from rela-tionships that extend beyond their own limits" (5).

One of the important consequences of this post-Heideggerian philosophy is that it breaks free of the *correlationism* mentioned earlier. Bogost explains, "units not only define people, network routers, genes, and electrical appliances, but also emotions, cultural symbols, business processes, and subjective experiences" (5).

Transitioning to the second term, Bogost begins by stating that units and systems are not opposed. Depending on the scale at which we are studying a phenomenon, we can scale up and read a system as a single unit, or we can scale down and choose any of the units in the aggregate for a "closer" analysis—or scale down even further from that unit-as-system to another aggregate within one of the units in the original aggregate. Compared to complex networks, systems "seek to explain all things via an unalieneable order" (6).

Finally, an operation is a "basic process" or rule. It is "the means by which something executes some purposeful action. In a programming language, an operation would be function that takes one or more inputs and performs a transformation on it" (7). Operations can be mechanical, tactical or discursive.

Based on these definitions, Bogost returns to the oppositional pair with which he started his chapter. He writes, "unit operations are creative, whereas systems operations are static. In the language of software engineering, unit operations are procedural, whereas system operations are structured" (8). The implications of this discussion about unit and systems operations have a direct bearing on his theory of ontography. Bogost will base his theory of ontography on the extent to which each ontographic species can participate in a creative dynamic.

In the following excerpt, Bogost explains why ontography has value:

> From the perspective of metaphysics, ontography involves the revelation of object relationships without necessarily offering clarification or description of any kind. Like a medieval bestiary, ontography can take the form of a compendium, a record of things juxtaposed to demonstrate their overlap and imply interaction through collocation. (38)

He follows up this explanation with a three-part taxonomy of ontographs. The first is the "inventory ontograph," which Bogost also calls a "Latour litany" and even more simply a list. The second is the visual or photographic ontograph. The third is the "ontographic machine" (*Alien* 35).

Of the first kind of ontograph, Bogost explains that a listing object is the "most basic form" of ontography (39). It is an "aesthetic set theory" in which a configuration is celebrated for the ways in which it "outs" the

Onto-Allegories for the 'Great Outdoors'

objects from their correlationist constraints. Bogost continues, "Lists are perfect tools to free us from the prison of representation precisely because they are so inexpressive" (*Alien* 40). Instead of describing the logic or uses or causal binder that joins a set of objects together, the "gentle knot" of the comma is used, which simultaneously separates clearly and loosely associates the members of the set.

According to Bogost, examples of this ontographic approach appear regularly in works by Bruno Latour and Harman. Bogost calls the former "Latour litanies," and offers several examples from which the following two are excerpted:

> A storm, a rat, a rock, a lake, a lion, a child, a worker, a gene, a slave, the unconscious, a virus.
>
> Elections, mass demonstrations, books, miracles, viscera laid open on the altar, viscera laid out on the operating table, figures, diagrams and plans, cries, monsters, exhibitions at the pillory. (*Alien* 38)

Bogost also cites Harman's use of lists. Two of the several that he cites include the following: "object-oriented philosophy holds that the relation of humans to pollen, oxygen, eagles, or windmills is no different in kind from the interaction of these objects with each other ... For we ourselves, just like Neanderthals, sparrows, mushrooms, and dirt, have never done anything else than act amidst the bustle of other actants" (*Alien* 39).

"Litanies are not indulgences," Bogost states, echoing Harman's own defense of his use of lists. In *Prince of Networks*, Harman rebuts the anticipated counter-argument, arguing that while some readers may characterize his use of lists as incantatory, or as a poetics of objects, "most readers will not soon grow tired, since the rhetorical power of these rosters of beings stems from their direct opposition to the flaws of current mainstream philosophy" (*Alien* 39). The flaws to which he alludes are the correlationist tendencies that lists are supposed to counter.

Digressing momentarily, lists can be further valued in relation to rhetorical style. First, they can be defined stylistically as *asyndeta*. *Silva Rhetorica* defines the scheme or figure, asyndeton, as "the omission of conjunctions between clauses, often resulting in a hurried rhythm or vehement effect" ("Scheme"). Jeanne Fahnestock mentions that it is one of the few about which Aristotle writes in Book III of his *Rhetoric*. Aristotle writes:

> *Asyndeta* have a special characteristic; many things seem to be said at the same time; for the connective makes many things seem one, so that if it is taken away, clearly the opposite results: one thing will be

many. Asyndeton thus creates amplification [*auxesis*]: "I came; I spoke; I besought" (these things seem many). (qtd. in Fahnestock 26)

Fahnestock follows up this quote explaining that if polysyndeton "emphasizes the act of joining, and correspondingly highlights each individual item linked together, then removing all conjunctions emphasizes the accumulation. The items spill out in a rush" (248). Her characterization of the items spilling out is a compelling depiction of the post-correlationist effect that this first kind of ontograph can have.

As Bogost has argued in *Alien Phenomenology*, the list is supposed to extricate objects from the correlationist confines in which they have been held. Along with the objects, the asyndenta allow something of the "great outdoors" to spill out, too. But more to Fahnestock's point, the accumulative character of lists, the "rush" to which they contribute, can be linked to another rhetorical figure, namely *climax*. It may not be a conventional notion of climax, in which items are implicitly linked an amplification, but there is a cumulative effect in their use, nonetheless. Finally, climax as a persuasive "unit" is one in which the centrifugal force of change is apparent.

The second "unit" in Bogost's taxonomy is the visual ontograph. Two of the examples that he details are François Blanciak's project titled *Siteless,* and a type of diagram known as an exploded-view drawing. Beginning with Blanciak, *Siteless* is a published book comprising 1,001 hand-drawn "building forms" that were inspired by five cities that he'd visited: Hong Kong, New York, Copenhagen, Los Angeles, and Tokyo. In the introduction to *Siteless,* Blanciak writes about an "expanding gap" between "morphological originality" in design and architectural research, which, by focusing almost exclusively on writing, ignores "experimentation and manipulation of form" (6). *Siteless* is also wordless, offering little more than a series of forms inspired by the aforementioned cities.

In order to achieve many of Blanciak's forms, new building techniques and materials would need to be invented. In the meantime, the forms, unconstrained by site, program, or budget, are invitations to explore new possibilities. From an ontographical standpoint, Blanciak challenges us to "reverse engineer" the alien cityscape in which any one of his forms could fit. What would the site and the urban plan or program be for any one of these forms? Bogost writes, "All together, the 1,001 takes on simultaneous abstract objects provide ontographies of unrelated objects, akin to Latour litanies but with implied if speculative material couplings between unfamiliar entities" (47).

Onto-Allegories for the 'Great Outdoors'

Turning to the exploded-view drawing, Bogost focuses on the various kinds of relations that define objects.

> To create an ontograph involves cataloging things, but also drawing attention to the couplings of and chasms between them. The tire and chassis, the ice milk and cup, the buckshot and soil: things like these exist not just for us but also for themselves and for one another, in ways that might surprise and dismay us. (*Alien* 50-51)

Bogost argues that the exploded-view diagram and the ontograph have "much in common" (52). The "configurative nature" of a thing or situation is foregrounded, offering a viewer a way of identifying the manifold unit operations in play.

The ontographic machine is the third and final species of ontography in Bogost's taxonomy. Compared to list and visual ontographs, ontographic machines do not merely imply, allude to, or even depict unit operations; rather, they are operational. Bogost offers several examples of ontographical machines. Initially, he divides his examples between abstract and concrete examples. Abstract ontographical machines include puzzle toys, such as Rubik's Cube, and games, such as *Tetris*. According to Bogost, abstract machines such as these are limited in their interactivity because they are "units removed from context such that their associations with other units becomes indistinct" (52). He doesn't make the following association, but we might extend his critique of these abstract games back to Blanciak's rectilinear forms, which, too, lack contextual or concrete meaning.

Concrete machines, on the other hand, combine "abstract gestures to concrete meanings," which Bogost values more highly. Two of the concrete, ontographic machines about which Bogost writes are the 2-D platform game, *Scribblenauts*, and the card game, *In a Pickle*. About *Scribblenauts*, Bogost offers the following introduction:

> The player controls a cute, pixelated character named Maxwell. Each of its two hundred levels takes place in an abstraction of a realistic environment, be it city, ice floe, mine, or ocean. Somewhere in the level sits a "Starite" (a shiny star icon), which the player must collect to complete the level. (*Alien* 53)

In the screen capture from *Scribblenauts* (see Figure 27), Maxwell will win a "Starite" by helping farmer Edwin clean and feed his pig. In order to help the player accomplish those tasks, the game prompts the player for words that will accomplish each task; so, typing "Clean the pig" will complete the first of several tasks.

Suasive Iterations

Figure 27. Screen capture of game play in *Scribblenauts*.

According to Bogost, the game's dictionary has over 22,000 words, and when a word appropriate for the situation is accepted by the game, the object or characteristic that the word represents is instantiated. For Bogost, the operational dimension of the words is tied to his interest in unit operations: "Scribblenauts . . . motivates players to explore a multitude of unit operations by sheer force of charm" (54).

Bogost's second example of a concrete ontographic machine is the card game, *In a Pickle* (see Figure 28). As with *Scribblenauts*, words in this card game are less centrally important for their denotative characteristics than their interoperationality. Latour litanies foreground the discreteness of objects in textual form, leading us to the "river of semiotic ontology" (56). *In a Pickle* foregrounds the manifold relations among objects based on the rhetorical conceit of *homography*. Bogost explains, "In linguistics, homographs are two different words that share the same orthography yet have different meanings" (57). The role of homography enables a player to relate the words or concepts on her cards in a wide range of ways. Bogost offers the following example:

> As the game title suggests, a Fork could be in a Pickle, but a Bank Robber could as well. For that matter, a Movie could be in a Pickle (when "Movie" is a metonym of its production), and yet a Pickle could be in a Movie (when "Pickle" is a prop). (57)

Onto-Allegories for the 'Great Outdoors'

Figure 28. Picture of *In a Pickle* card game.

Bogost contrasts a Latour litany, which is made from words, with *In a Pickle*, which is "a machine for producing ontographs *about* words" (58). *In a Pickle* is intriguing because it is a much more than a catalog of words. It is a catalog of what Bogost calls "the inside of words" (58). By "exploding the innards of things," Bogost concludes, we expose the many unit operations that have been hidden and dormant from within the confines of correlationism.

Bogost values all three species of ontograph for the ways in which they bring forth some of what has been occluded by correlationism. Each one is like an invitation to the "great outdoors," the experience of which Bogost described above as "a 'global ether' of incredible novelty and unfamiliarity" (Alien 38). Harkening back to my casuistic stretching of Rosenfield's approach to epideictic, Bogost's ontographical approach to the "great outdoors" could be repurposed as an inventional strategy for introducing an audience to the radiance of Being. Each ontograph brings out a different aspect of the post-correlationist world to which they are applied.

Bogost describes ontographs as a "general inscriptive strategy, one that uncovers the repleteness of units and their interobjectivity" (*Alien* 38), but his ontographs can be more than a representational technology. His ontographs can be valued as a form of writing, of being-writing. If, as Lanham argues, reality is not something "out there" that we passively apprehend, then ontographs can be far more than a "general inscriptive strategy, one that uncovers the repleteness of units and their interobjectivity" (38). Bogost's ontographs create realities—each one offering us a different composing process. From the standpoint of digital rhetoric in an era of physical computing, his ontographs are contributions to an inventional strategy for everting the conventional, correlationist experience. Combined with Lanham's attention-traps, his ontographs offer digital rhetors a method for making our conventional experience of reality more radiant or irridescent.

Onto-Allegorical Approach to UC

Lanham teaches us that attention is not a generic quantity, a commodity. He teaches us to rethink the drive toward clarity or calm in UC approaches to physical computing, and to replace that approach with the goal of creating attention-getting traps. Bogost teaches us that our conventional experience of reality is correlationist, and that there is a vast reality—a "great outdoors" waiting to be experienced, too. His ontographical approach is a way in which to write into our conventional experience of reality some of that post-correlationist reality.

When we combine Lanham's and Bogost's perspectives on attention and reality, respectively, we have the basis for what I call an *onto-allegorical* approach to digital rhetoric in the era of physical computing, an inventional approach related to the canon of style. Bogost's ontographs are a way of writing aspects of a post-correlationist reality into our lives, and the rhetorical goal of that approach to being-writing is to create an attention-getting, epideictic experience that suades an audience toward a digital experience that is not predicated on the conservative values of calm.

Onto-Allegories for the 'Great Outdoors'

My rereading of #Flock explains how an onto-allegorical approach might work. Chapter 3.5, which follows this one, offers a technical application of this proposal.

Onto-allegorizing #Flock so that some of the "dance of information" on Twitter's network is made expressive involves Twitter's application protocol interface, or API. An API is a software interface that offers developers limited access to a company's services. If a developer wants access to some of the information and services provided by a company, she would apply for access and then learn how to access the company's services through its API.

Thousands of web-based APIs are available. The ProgrammableWeb boasts a current list of over 13,000 web-based APIs. Most popular companies on the web have an API, including Amazon, Apple's iTunes, YouTube, AccuWeather, LinkedIn, Yahoo, Google, Pinterest, Instagram, Tumblr, and Facebook. As a point of reference, when you download an app for your mobile phone, the permissions that you accept are the basis for API calls to that company's services.

For most Twitter users, a tweet or "status update" is a fairly complex multimodal object. It is a 140-character message posted to their service. It can contain text, video, links, one or more @usernames and hashtagged words or phrases; also, it can be retweeted, replied to, and favorited.

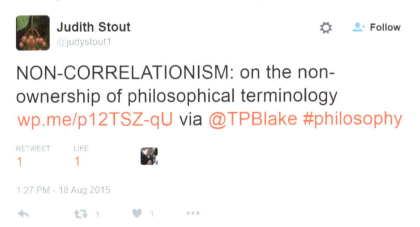

Figure 29. Sample tweet from a search for "correlationism."

Figure 29 is the screen capture of a tweet that was found when I searched "correlationism" at twitter.com. To the right of Judith Stout's profile picture is her name, @username, and a tweet, which includes a URL to a blog post, another @username, and a #keyword. The two 1s below that signify that @judystout1's tweet has been retweeted and favorited once each.

Suasive Iterations

For a rhetor exploring the onto-allegorical potential of Twitter's API, the same tweet takes on a higher level of complexity. The following is a printout of the same tweet (a "status") using the Twitter4J library for Processing.

StatusJSONImpl{createdAt=Tue Aug 18 13:27:37 EDT 2015, id=633691733008719872, text='NON-CORRELATIONISM: on the non-ownership of philosophical terminology http://t.co/4Sv71O-QaOJ via @TPBlake #philosophy', source='<a href="http://twitter.com" rel="nofollow">Twitter Web Client</a>', isTruncated=false, inReplyToStatusId=-1, inReplyToUserId=-1, isFavorited=false, isRetweeted=false, favoriteCount=1, inReplyToScreenName='null', geoLocation=null, place=null, retweetCount=1, isPossiblySensitive=-false, lang='en', contributorsIDs=[], retweetedStatus=null, userMentionEntities=[UserMentionEntityJSONImpl{name='Terence Blake', screenName='TPBlake', id=201402940}], urlEntities=[URLEntityJSONImpl{url='http://t.co/4Sv71OQaOJ', expandedURL='http://wp.me/p12TSZ-qU', displayURL='wp.me/p12TSZ-qU'}], hashtagEntities=[HashtagEntityJSONImpl{text='philosophy'}], mediaEntities=[], symbolEntities=[], currentUserRetweetId=-1, user=UserJSONImpl{id=416608486, name='Judith Stout', screenName='judystout1', location='usa', description='Music grad, married, seeking new thought patterns in changing world.Read Philosophy, Hist, Politics. Interested in everything', isContributorsEnabled=false, profileImageUrl= 'http://pbs.twimg.com/profile_images/2259272648/IMG0010_normal.jpg',profileImageUrlHttps='https://pbs.twimg.com/profile_images/2259272648/IMG0010_normal.jpg', isDefaultProfileImage=false, url='null', isProtected=false, followersCount=2950, status=null, profileBackgroundColor='C0DEED', profileTextColor='333333', profileLinkColor='0084B4', profileSidebarFillColor='DDEEF6', profileSidebarBorderColor='C0DEED', profileUseBackgroundImage= true, isDefaultProfile=true, showAllInlineMedia=false, friendsCount=2918, createdAt=Sat Nov 19 17:43:29 EST 2011, favouritesCount=18, utcOffset=-10800, timeZone='Atlantic Time (Canada)', profileBackgroundImageUrl= 'http://abs.twimg.com/images/themes/theme1/bg.png', profileBackgroundImageUrlHttps='https://abs.twimg.com/images/themes/theme1/bg.png', profileBackgroundTiled=false, lang='en', statusesCount=34504, isGeoEnabled=false, isVerified=false, translator=false, listedCount=120, isFollowRequestSent=false, withheldInCountries=null}, withHeldInCountries=null}

Onto-Allegories for the 'Great Outdoors'

Beginning in the middle of the second line and continuing to the middle of the fourth is the tweet, "NON-CORRELATIONISM: on the non-ownership of philosophical terminology http://t.co/4Sv71OQaOJ via @TPBlake #philosophy." It is 118 characters long, including the white spaces. In contrast, the entire status object quoted above is 2196 characters in length, which is more than 18 times longer than her tweet. Far more telling than its size, however, is the status' complexity as a computational object. First, there are numerous types of data bundled together. There are strings, which are textual. Strings in the status above include text, description, lang, and name. Several types of numbers appear, including integers, hexadecimals, and long numbers. Integer data types that are standard in length include retweetCount, favoritesCount, and followersCount. Long integers include id, inReplyToUserId, and currentUserRetweetId. All of the profile colors are hexadecimal numbers. There are Booleans (true or false), including isTruncated, isFavorited, isContributorsEnabled, and isDefaultProfile.

In addition to the above-described data types are several more that are unique to Twitter. In the status, there are five types of entities listed. They are userMentionEntities, urlEntities, hashtagEntities, mediaEntities, and symbolEntities. Whenever a tweet includes an @screenname, a url, one or more #hashtags, media (sound, image, or video), or $symbols, they are stored as unique entities. For example, when @judystout1 cites @TPBlake, the latter @screenname is redefined as userMentionEntity.

userMentionEntities=[UserMentionEntityJSONImpl{name='Terence Blake', screenName='TPBlake', id=201402940}]

The complexity of this aspect of the status is signified by the use of the opening and closing square brackets (the [and]) , the opening and closing "curly braces" (the { and }), and the three coma-delimited statements contained within them, the first one of which is "name='Terence Blake'." The brackets, braces, commas, and equal signs are expressive of a complex, computational structure—one that is effaced by the "user-friendly" tweet displayed on the screen.

Onto-allegorizing those and other aspects of the computational structure of a status is a way of foregrounding the "great outdoors" of Twitter's application environment. It is a way of expressing some of the dance of information that is otherwise hidden behind the user-friendly interface at twitter.com or on any number of other twitter client apps. We can interrogate the output above from the Twitter API using Bogost's three types of ontographs. Beginning with the list ontograph, one way in which to proceed is to generate a "word cloud" of the above-quoted tweet that includes all of the technical language from the back-end data type. Figure 30 is the output from Dan Bernier's Processing-based library called WordCram. The hexadecimal profile colors in the status object are used to colorize the text in the cloud. The most prominent text element in the cloud is the Boolean value, false. The text from the tweet is nowhere to be found; the outdoors is front and center.

Figure 30. A word cloud of the tweet cited above.

The second of Bogost's ontographical types—the visual ontograph—is one for which the goal is to highlight the relations comprising an object, "drawing attention to the couplings of the chasms between them" (50-51). His example of this kind of ontograph is the exploded-view diagram. One way to develop a visual ontograph of the Twitter status above is to recreate it as a three-dimensional object in Processing. The various parts of the status object—from "createdAt" to "withHeldInCountries"—could be linked together with lines simulating a wire frame. As new statuses are recorded by Processing, the values associated with each of the status elements could be updated, the object turning slowly on one or more axes as a way of allegorizing stylistically the "weight" of the information it has stored.

For Bogost, it is the third type of ontograph that he finds most compelling, but I am not sure that I agree—not when the goal is to allegorize some aspect of Twitter's cloud-like structure. A more compelling way forward is to combine some of the defamiliarizing aspects of the first type of ontograph with an allegorization of its exploded view. If the complex, multi-dimensional structure of a status or tweet can be foregounded, there is an opportunity to foreground its structure over and above the text of the

Onto-Allegories for the 'Great Outdoors'

tweet. With the right kind of physical computing project, some of the complexity of the tweet-as-object can be allegorized, which can lead to the kind of attention-getting disturbance that is needed to evert the faceless truth of UC's correlationist calm.

3.5 Onto-Allegorized Tweets and the Third (Wayve) State

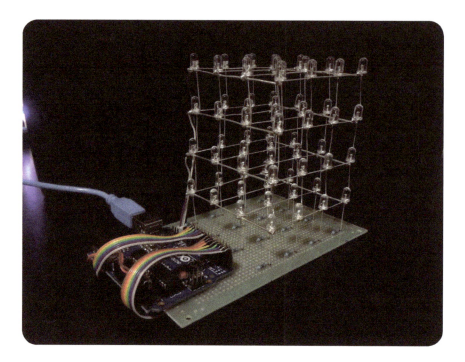

Figure 31. An Arduino-driven, charlieplexed 4x4x4 LED Cube. Photo credit: Michael Chen.

Sixty-four LEDs, nine 120-Ohm resistors, an Arduino UNO, and a lot of solder—a list of technologies for disturbing the peace. In YouTube videos, LED cubes can be programmed to cycle through complex visualizations that simulate everything from balls of light bouncing around 3D space to wave-like sheets that appear to ripple and twist. The goal of this project is to develop an LED cube that transduces some of the hidden structure of a tweet into a conspicuous visual allegorization.

Unbeknownst to the average Twitter user is the multi-dimensional depth and breadth of information with which a tweet is associated. For the average user, a tweet is 140 characters long, it can include images and video, and it can be replied to and retweeted. But there is a vast array of data associated with each and every tweet. If a physical computing project is developed that visualizes some of the hidden data fields associated with an incoming

Onto-Allegorized Tweets and the Third (Wayve) State

tweet, there is the possibility of everting some of what is usually hidden into what Craig Saper, writing as dj readies, calls an intimately bureaucratic experience: "a paradoxical mix of artisanal production, mass-distribution techniques, and a belief in the democratizing potential of social media" (1).

As I explained in Chapters 2 and 3, one reason the era of physical computing is able to serve us so well is that it is busily engaged in a distal, post-correlationist "dance of information" of which we are supposed to be unaware. To the extent that the hidden structure of a tweet can be allegorized visually and kinetically in as conspicuous an object as an LED cube, some of that "great outdoors" may be brought within our field of concern.

In Chapter 3, I wrote about #Flock, an Arduino-based physical computing project that sits on its owner's desk or bookshelf. It was designed to celebrate Twitter, but it serves well as an encalming technology.

Figure 32. #Flock. Photo credit: Oran O'Reilly.

Even while its owner's Twitter feed may be active with endless updates, #Flock sits quietly. The only times it reacts are when its owner gains a new follower, has a message retweeted, or receives an @message, at which point one of three mechanical birds emerge to sing a song. #Flock is an engaging project, and the ways in which it brings together the legacy of cuckoo clocks with the Twitter bird is creative and compelling. In fact, the avian mash-up can be valued as a type of attention-getting structures about which

Suasive Iterations

Lanham has written; however, the project also contributes to a legacy of anti-rhetorical calls for calm. Based on the ways in which it contributes to the kind of truth about which Nietzsche wrote, the goal of the project in this chapter is to create another kind of desktop object that is both attention-getting, and which allegorizes stylistically some of Twitter's "bureaucracy."

The inventional process for this particular project is somewhat more complicated than the one followed in Chapter 2.5 because the process of transduction involves a complex actuator, an LED cube, and a more complicated array of data than the one in Chapter 2.5. Beginning with stages 1 and 2 of the inventional process, we need to develop a technical understanding of both objects and the data ranges with which they are associated.

LED cubes are technically challenging to create for several reasons. First, they require the patience to solder together 4 two-dimensional layers of 16 LEDs each, which will be stacked to create a 4x4x4 cube. That process alone requires nearly 200 blobs of solder to secure everything properly. Second, all of the anode (positive) and cathode (negative or ground) legs on each of the LEDs must be properly bent and aligned for soldering in order to create the complex, two-dimensional electrical circuit that winds up and around the three-dimensions of the cube. Third, each of the four lines of soldered anode legs comprising a vertical column, and each of the horizontal rows of cathode legs need to be connected to pins on the Arduino. Those pins need to be properly labeled in preparation for coding. Additionally, resistors need to be included in the circuit because, if the Arduino writes too much electricity to the circuit, the LEDs will burn out. Finally, a software program needs to be written that can turn on and off one or more LEDs in looping sequences based on a charlieplexed network of 64 actuators (the LEDs).

Charlieplexing is a type of "display multiplexing." It is named after Charlie Allen, who helped develop it at Maxim Integrated in the mid-1990s. Charlieplexing solves an important issue, which is how to control dozens or more outputs from a small number of pins. Solving that issue is both practical and economical. On a practical level, few microcontrollers will have as many as 64 pins to power each of the LEDs in a 4x4x4. And if someone wanted to create an even larger cube, like the 16x16x16 cube in Figure 33, they would need 4096 pins.

Onto-Allegorized Tweets and the Third (Wayve) State

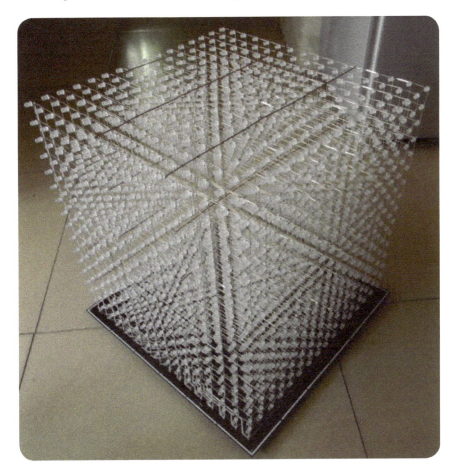

Figure 33. A 16x16x16 LED cube. Photo credit: Mike Neuhaus

Even if there were a microcontroller with 4096 pins, it is not an efficient use of hardware, processing power or electrical energy. For this reason, Charlieplexing is an efficient and clever way in which to proceed.

Charlieplexing relies on the "three-state" or "tri-state" logic of microcontrollers like the Arduino. For novice Arduino programmers working with LEDs, a digital pin's mode must be set to OUTPUT and then it can be set to one of two states, HIGH or LOW. Sketches like "Blink" reinforce this assumption. But several pins on an Arduino offer rhetors a third (wayve) state. When they are set to INPUT, they become open. Technically, it means that they are in a state of high impedance. For all intents and purposes, the pin has been disconnected from the circuit. To put it figuratively, the sections of a circuit that are associated with an open pin have been ghosted—they have been "disappeared." Their openness along with the uni-directional flow of electricity through an LED makes it possible to design a complex matrix of electrical flows using fewer pins; therefore, 9 pins is all that is needed to run a 4x4x4 cube. The formula for determining how many pins will be needed for a given number of LEDs is the following: you need n pins to control $n*(n-1)$ LEDs. For a 4x4x4 LED cube comprising 64 LEDs, you will need 9 pins.

Moving on to Twitter, Figure 34 is an exploded diagram of the StatusJSONImpl object in the Twitter API. The diagram should be read from left to right. JSON is an acronym for "JavaScript Object Notation." It is a popular standard for structuring data. In the Twitter API, a status is another name for a tweet. "Impl" is an abbreviation for implementation. The StatusJSONImpl is a complex, hierarchical data structure for tweets.

To the right of StatusJSONImpl are 26 object properties, from "createdAt" at the top to "user" approximately halfway down Figure 34. Those properties represent a variety of data types including strings, long integers, arrays (represented by the "[]"), colors, and URLs. Of the seven arrays, several have additional, lower-level properties associated with them. UserMentionEntities[] opens out to a property titled UserMentionEntity-JSONImpl, and then three more, name, screenName, and id. Below symbolEntities[], user opens out to 37 more properties, from id to withHeldInCountries. Compared to the three dimensions of accelerometer data on which the project in Chapter 2.5 was based—all three of which had the same range (0-1024)—this Twitter object is far more complex. While its complexity may be intimidating, the possibilities for transducing and then allegorizing some of the data associated with it are wide-ranging.

Moving on to stage 3, the focus here is on some of the data fields found in the StatusJSONImpl object. With the ultimate goal of allegorizing some of the hidden bureaucracy within a tweet, there are a number of fields on which to focus. Our list of transducible fields can include the following:

geoLocation, place, or location
timeZone
retweetCount
followersCount
friendsCount
lang
profileBackgroundColor

Onto-Allegorized Tweets and the Third (Wayve) State

StatusJSONImpl	createdAt=		
	id=		
	text=		
	source=		
	isTruncated=		
	inReplyToStatusId=		
	inReplyToUserId=		
	isFavorited=		
	isRetweeted=		
	favoriteCount=		
	inReplyToScreenName=		
	geoLocation=		
	place=		
	retweetCount=		
	isPossiblySensitive=		
	lang=		
	retweetedStatus=		
	currentUserRetweetId=		
	withHeldInCountries=		
	contributorsIDs=[]		
	userMentionEntities=[	UserMentionEntityJSONImpl	name= screenName= id=]
	urlEntities=[	URLEntityJSONImpl	url= expandedURL= displayURL=]
	hashtagEntities[	HashtagEntityJSONImpl	Text=]
	mediaEntities=[]		
	symbolEntities=[]		
	user=UserJSONImpl[	id=	
		name=	
		screenName=	
		location=	
		description=	
		isContributorsEnabled=	
		profileImageUrl=	
		isDefaultProfileImage=	
		url=	
		isProtected=	
		followersCount=	
		status=	
		profileBackgroundColor=	
		profileTextColor=	
		profileLinkColor=	
		profileSidebarFillColor=	
		profileSidebarBorderColor=	
		profileUseBackgroundImage=	
		isDefaultProfile=	
		showAllInLineMedia=	
		friendsCount=	
		Created At=	
		favouritesCount=	
		utcOffset=	
		timeZone=	
		profileBackgroundImageUrl=	
		profileBackgroundImageUrlHttps=	
		profileBackgroundTiled=	
		lang=	
		statusesCount=	
		isGeoEnabled=	
		isVerified=	
		Translator=	
		listedCount=	
		isFollowRequestSent=	
		withheldInCountries=	

Figure 34. Hierarchical structure of @dmrieder's status or tweet.

This list is partial. You can pull from most any of the fields, albeit some of the fields in a given instance of the StatusJSONImpl object may by null or otherwise unavailable. For example, if a user associated with a tweet that you've received has their geoLocation turned off, you will not have access to their place or location. But if any or all of these fields are turned on,

Suasive Iterations

it would be possible to transduce and then allegorize visually the data associated with it. For example, you might blink the LED Cube as many times as the number associated with retweetCount or followersCount, or turn on patterned sequences of LEDs to allegorize the number. You could generate a visualization that allegorizes the timeZone, or the preferred lang(uage) associated with a retweet. The timeZone could be allegorized as an hour hand within the LED cube.

Expanding on the above-mentioned ideas for allegorizing visually the data associated with StatusJSONImpl, stage 4 of the inventional process could focus exclusively on the number of users, friends, and followers associated with a given tweet. In other words, the cube could be used to allegorize the depth or complexity of the network of users connected to an incoming tweet or retweet. One approach could be the following: divide the LED cube among four cuboids; assign three of them to data fields associated with a user's followers, friends, and retweets; assign the fourth to a user's time zone or geolocation. The following is list of the four allegorizations:

Dim/brighten a quadrant of the cube to visualize a user's followersCount
Dim/brighten a quadrant of the cube to visualize a user's friendsCount
Dim/brighten a quadrant of the cube to visualize the number of retweets
Dim/brighten a quadrant of the cube to visualize a user's timeZone or geoLocation

There are a wide range of possibilities for visualizing the data. This is just one possible way forward.

Moving on to stage 5, the visualization dashboard for this project is a little more involved than the one in Chapter 2.5. In this visualization, there are two views, which offer digital rhetors different ways in which to identify, conceptualize, and brainstorm approaches to both transduction and allegorization. Figure 35 is a screen capture of the first view, a list ontograph of an incoming tweet to my Twitter account. It is rendered as a tag-cloud using the WordCram library for Processing.

Onto-Allegorized Tweets and the Third (Wayve) State

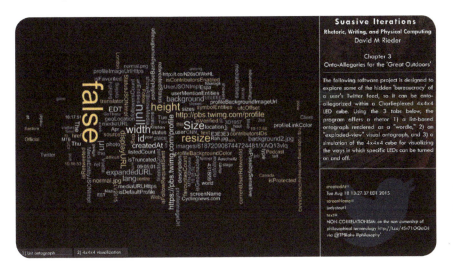

Figure 35. "List ontograph" as tag cloud of an incoming tweet

The advantage of using the Wordle library in Processing to visualize an incoming tweet (and its structure) is that it can help recognize the kind of data with which you can work.

The second view is a simulation of a 4x4x4 LED cube (see figure 36). The simulation is designed to make it easier to learn the structure of the cube in order to test kinetic sequences for onto-allegorical visualizations. The simulation in the Processing sketch can be rotated in three dimensions, and it can be moved back and forth on the z dimension. The goal of the third point of view is to learn how to turn on/off specific LEDs, and then to learn how to turn on/off patterns of LEDs in the actual cube. By changing the fill color of one or more LED images in the simulation, and then rotating the cube around, you can develop a stronger sense of the structure on which the charlieplexing is based.

Suasive Iterations

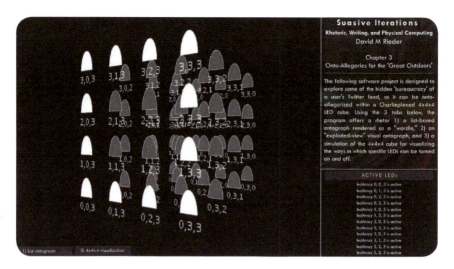

Figure 36. LED cube simulator in Processing

By changing the 0s, 1s, and 2s associated with the three-dimensional array of LED images, you can play around with turning on and off patterns of lights. Once you have developed a stronger sense of how to turn on and off LEDs within the simulated cube, the software program can be rewritten so that it works with the LED cube that you have soldered together.

On a concluding note, since the goal of this project is to disturb the peace, one or more speakers could be included for added effect. The speakers could be used to play sound samples. For example, they could play a constant range of sounds associated with the radio signals recorded by the SETI project, to equate the "alienated" aspects of a tweet with the search for extra-human or post-correlationist life in the "great outdoors."

4 Plumbing the Paradoxical Depths

Figure 37. emBody(Text){ at the Sixty-Third Annual Conventional for Communication and Composition (CCCC), St. Louis.

For three days in late March, 2012, Kevin Brock's and my Kinect-based digital interactive work, emBody(Text){, was on display at the St. Louis Convention Center. Hundreds of conference attendees passed by the hallway wall on which the work was projected, and as groups large and small walked past it, their 20-foot tall, textualized silhouettes would follow. Some conference-goers walked by unaware of the textualized silhouette following them down the hall. Others took notice, slowing down or stopping. Some of those who stopped tried to read their textual silhouettes, looking for meaning, while others engaged with its kinetic, dynamic character. This latter group was far fewer in number, but they were one of my favorite audiences. They might stop to sway back and forth in front of the wall, move their arms up and down, or even dance with their textualized avatar for a few seconds before giggling and walking away. Children, too, engaged with their silhouettes. They cared little for the meaning of the texts (they didn't try to read them) but were engaged with some of the works' instant feedback—by what can be described as the real-time transduction of their shape, position, and movements into an everting and rhetorically-engaging event. They laughed, jumped, and ran around. They were enthralled by the everted facsimile of their shape and movements—and their excitement inevitably drew in a few more adults. It was in those moments—moments of epideictic rhetoric—when I realized what technologies like the Kinect offered digital rhetors. These technologies enabled us to reconnect with some of the lost arts of delivery, but to do so by exploring the body in new ways.

For over a half-century, natural-user interface (NUI) design has increasingly implicated the entire body of a user into computer systems. There are several interrelated histories that comprise this "long nose" of innovation, and they are usually related to the ways in which we sense and act on the world. There are separate histories for finger touch, eye, voice, arm and hand gesture, and what has been called full body computing. Consumer technologies such as Apple's iPad, Microsoft's Kinect, and Google Glass are the culmination of long histories of innovation. The ubiquitous touch-screen, for example, which in rhetorical terms could be associated with *dactylogical* forms of delivery, has been available since the early 1970s (see Figure 38). In the present moment, not only is the body at the cutting-edge of computational research related to NUI, but indeed it has been in development for decades.

Figure 38. PLATO IV Terminal (1972-1974). Photo credit: University of Illinois Archive.

Plumbing the Paradoxical Depths

Meanwhile, in our present moment in rhetoric, most of the scholarship associated with the recent revival of interest in the fifth canon of delivery appears to have "doubled down" on perpetuating a disembodied approach to rhetoric. In the past twenty years, rhetoric scholars have contributed to a revitalization of the fifth canon, but they have done so by sidestepping what Ben McCorkle calls the "body-centric notion of delivery" (2). In the place of the body, two predominate new approaches are to redefine delivery as the design of print and digital documents (Pullman; Bodmer; Ridolfo and DeVoss), and as various forms of distributed or circulated media across various kinds of communication networks and workflow processes (Trimbur; Yancey; Brooke). There are other approaches, but these two stand out.

This is not to argue that digital delivery defined in terms of document design and what Jim Ridolfo has called the "strategic movement" of texts was not an innovative move because it certainly was. Arguably, after the "linguistic turn," a persistently linguistic and textual bias in humanities scholarship marginalized the body for decades; so, considering those rhetorical constraints, reconceptualizing delivery as design and dissemination was innovative. But from the standpoint of NUI innovation, the absence of the gesturing body in a revived canon of digital delivery is conspicuous. In the emerging post-PC era in which new approaches to human-computer interfaces have become a cutting-edge for research and design, the human body is the interface. It is time to resuscitate the body-centric approach to delivery, updating it for the brave new NUI era in which we increasingly find ourselves in our everyday lives.

In this chapter, the NUI technology upon which a return to the body will be based is Microsoft's first-generation Kinect, which was initially released in November of 2010. There is a Version 2 sensor, which is known as the Kinect One, but many more easy-to-learn, open source projects have been developed for the first-generation sensor. Development environments for the original sensor have been established for Windows, Apple, and Linux; so, it is a more broadly established platform for innovation than the Kinect One.

When the original Kinect sensor was released, it was sold as a peripheral for the XBOX 360. Kinect for XBOX 360 was marketed as the first "hands-free" gaming system. The tag line for the sensor was, "You are the controller." It soon became the most popular peripheral on the market. In March of 2011, after selling more than 8 million units in 60 days, it had surpassed Apple's iPad and iPhone in the same period of time. In the spring of 2011, *Guinness World Records* awarded the Kinect the title of "fastest-selling consumer electronics device on record" ("Fastest-selling"). In February 2013, 26 months after its release, Microsoft had sold over 24 million units.

For mainstream users, the Kinect's success is based largely on its ability to identify and track the position and movements of several users in real time. It is also known for its location-aware, voice-actuated capabilities; it can associate a voice with a specific player, based on her tracked position in the game space. An example of its body-tracking capabilities is in an advertisement for *Kinect Adventures!*, a game comprising twenty individual levels that is bundled with the sensor. In an advertisement for the game (see Figure 39), a woman is depicted bending forward at her hips and knees, her arms are outstretched behind her and feet pointing forward. On the screen in front of her, an avatar is negotiating an obstacle course. The position of the avatar's hips, knees, arms, and feet mirror those of the player.

Figure 39. Woman playing *Kinect Adventures!* Photo credit: Microsoft Corp.

If one or more players jump, spin around, kick a leg in the air, or point a foot in a different direction, the sensor will track the changes, mapping each of those movements onto their on-screen avatars. This is the basis for playing soccer, baseball, or boxing, driving a racecar, performing yoga poses, and dancing.

While its explicit, body-centric approach to gaming and its global success are two compelling reasons to focus on the Kinect in a chapter on

Plumbing the Paradoxical Depths

NUI, a more salient reason is the way in which it became an open-source platform for scores of innovative projects. By December of 2010, a month after the Kinect was released, the sensor had been transformed into an experimental platform for open and innovative work in the arts, engineering, and education. It began the day the Kinect was released, when Limon Fried (aka Lady Ada) and Phillip Torrone of AdaFruit Industries sponsored a competition that they called the Open Kinect Prize, or OK Prize. They stated that they would award $3000 to the first person to develop open source drivers for the Kinect sensor. In the announcement for the contest on their blog, team Adafruit included the following explanations for their contest:

> What do we (all) want?
> Open source drivers for this cool USB device, the drivers and/or application can run on any operating system—but completely documented and under an open source license. To demonstrate the driver you must also write an application with one "window" showing video (640 x 480) and one window showing depth. Upload all of this to GitHub.
>
> How get the bounty ($3,000 USD)
> Anyone around the world can work on this, including Microsoft ☺
> Upload your code, examples and documentation to GitHub. First person / group to get RGB out with distance values being used wins, you're smart—you know what would be useful for the community out there. All the code needs to be open source and/or public domain. Email us a link to the repository, we and some "other" *Kinect* for Xbox 360 hackers will check it out—if it's good to go, you'll get the $3,000 bounty! ("The Open *Kinect* project")

On November 10, less than a week after the *Kinect*'s North American release, Lady Ada announced that Hector Matin Cantero, aka marcan, had won the prize. Marcan was already known for his support of the Linux OS as well as for several other "hacks," including one related to the security systems for the PlayStation 3. Marcan won the competition when he posted to GitHub a rudimentary Linux-based driver that streamed RGB and depth data from the Kinect to an OpenGL application. His "hack" would eventually be named libfreenect. It was the basis for the Open Kinect initiative.

Following on the heels of the OK Prize was a second open-source initiative. In December 2010, a group called OpenNI released a set of open-source drivers for the Kinect as well as an API for software development. The differences between the two initiatives are important. Whereas the Open Kinect drivers were initially focused on the RGB image and depth data streams, the OpenNI drivers and API offered RGB, depth, and joint data. As developers chose sides, the key point of comparison between the two initiatives was that one offered joint data.

By the end of 2010, the Kinect had become a powerful, experimental platform for interdisciplinary research and DIY project development. A testament to its success is the website *Kinect Hacks*, which debuted in December 2010. Since its debut, the site has hosted hundreds of sample projects from established academic labs, art collectives, start-ups, and individual "tinkerers." The Open Kinect and OpenNI websites also host scores of sample projects.

Based in part on the Kinect's successes as an open technology, in the spring of 2011 Microsoft announced that it, too, would release a set of drivers and an SDK for Windows-based project development; they released them that June. The next year, in February 2012, Microsoft released a Version 2 Kinect sensor (the Kinect One) specifically designed for Windows development, and the early "beta" version of their SDK was replaced by an official Version 1.

For digital rhetors, the Kinect's status as an open-source platform is a significant opportunity to expand the canon of digital delivery, especially by reengaging with its "body-centric" history. It is an opportunity to transform aspects of the long history of *gestus* that Marcus Fabius Quintilianus (Quintilian) helped inaugurate in the eleventh book of his *Institutio Oratoria*. In particular, it is an opportunity to move beyond a representational or instrumental approach to the body, which has predominated the discourse associated with the canon. The ways in which a body can be redefined computationally by the Kinect are numerous. Those redefinitions of the body are based on eversions of the boundary between a sensed body and its projected feedback in an event space. A revamped fifth canon that focuses on (re)delivering a participant's body back to her as an everted relation would better reflect the new era of Kinect-based NUI programming.

In order to promote the Kinect as an experimental platform for both digital delivery and digital writing, the remainder of this chapter is divided among three sections. The first section is a brief history of rhetoric's approach to gesture and other embodied forms of expression in relation to the fifth canon. The second section is a review of the some of the ways in which contemporary theorists outside of rhetoric have reconceptualized what gestures and embodied movement are in a generative or creative sense. The third section is a general introduction to NUI, followed by a technical review of the Kinect's capabilities.

Plumbing the Paradoxical Depths

Rhetoric's Uneasy Relation with Gesture

From Aristotle's early assessments to its eventual decline in value in the late-18th century, rhetoric has had an ambivalent relationship to human gestures and other forms of embodied movement. Gesturing, posturing, and other forms of embodied expression are essential, but they must be refined and their role limited and subordinated to the rhetor's speech. Simply put, the body must be tamed.

In his book *Gesture: Visible Action as Utterance*, Adam Kendon helps us recognize the persistent ambivalence with which rhetoricians have treated the body. He begins with the following assessment: "In the Western tradition, among the Greeks and, later, the Romans, gesture was recognized as a feature of human expression, that being powerful, must be shaped and regulated in accordance with the aims of creating persuasive or effective discourse" (17). Kendon argues that for Aristotle, a rhetor's gestures were recognized as a powerful way in which to "sway the feelings of the crowds," but the simple fact that they did not directly serve the "principles of reason" meant that they should be regulated (17). Kendon continues, explaining that in both Cicero's and Quintilian's treatments of delivery, the movements of the body are more highly regarded; nonetheless, they are reduced to a subordinate role.

Citing Nico Lamedica's scholarship, Kendon explains how, for Cicero, gestures—especially facial ones—"were to be used to express the feelings that lie behind a discourse," and that they "should be employed in a measured and dignified fashion" (17). Echoing Cicero's approach, in Quintilian's theory of *gestus*, gestures of the hands, body, and face serve the voice of the speaker. In his summary of key passages of the final section of Book XI of Quintilian's *Institutio Oratoria*, which Kendon calls the "most complete discussion of gesture from the Roman era," allusions to the subordination of body movements to speech are apparent: "According to Quintilian, and here he follows Cicero, the orator uses gestures to convey the force of what is being said and to indicate the objects of his thought, but not as a substitute for what he says in words" (19).

According to Kendon, Quintilian's discussion of *gestus* is relatively short, and its impact on the generation of rhetors during which it was published is clear. It would, however, become highly influential by the end of the sixteenth century, when the value of gesturing in the canon of delivery would be elevated.

By the start of the seventeenth century, several influences had coalesced to "elevate" the role of the fifth canon and of gesturing. One factor, which had been building since the mid-fifteenth century, was the discovery of full manuscripts of Quintilian's treatise as well as several lost treatises by

Cicero during the middle ages. During the middle ages, rhetoric training had been focused on intellectual pursuits. As a full picture was reconstructed of the early Roman approach to rhetoric, "rhetoric came to be seen as a matter of practical import as well as of intellectual training" (Kendon 20). The early Romans promoted the ideal of the orator as both "philosopher and a man of action of high moral integrity," who was fully involved in politics (20). Another factor that raised the role of gesturing in rhetoric was due to changes in religious services and ceremonies. In the Protestant, Catholic, and later Jesuit traditions, the importance of the sermon would add the role of teacher to that of preacher. Kendon writes, "The priest became a persuader as well as a manager of ritual" (21). Finally, Peter Ramus's influential reduction of rhetoric to elocution (style) and delivery elevated the latter during the early modern period.

Of the many treatises published during that century, Kendon cites two that had a lasting influence: Giovanni Bonifacio's *L'Arte de' Cenni*, and John Bulwer's *Chirologia*. Kendon claims that the works by Bonifacio and Bulwer "are the most often recalled today" (22). In both texts, gesture is treated in great detail, but it is reduced to a subordinate role, serving either voice or the ideas implied in a speech. About Bonifacio, Kendon relays the following assessment:

> [Bonifacio] believed that bodily signs reveal more clearly and truthfully than words a person's feelings and intentions. At the same time, however, he believed that if one can master the art of using the body to make signs one can control the impression that one makes on other people. (23)

Mastery and control qualify the natural and powerful role of gesturing. Writing about Bulwer's detailed treatments of gestures once again, Kendon explains that the body's expressivity is regulated and reduced to a subordinate role:

> Bulwer is concerned to show that the artistic use of gesture must be founded upon the natural. The meanings of the gestures employed have their justification in their natural origins, but their employment must be carefully regulated by the requirements of appropriateness, grace, and decorum. (27)

After the decline of oratory during the modern period, the fifth canon would all but disappear, along with the canon of memory. But in the 1980s, rhetoric scholars would begin contributing to what is now lauded as a revival of the fifth canon—especially as the contributions focused on the

Plumbing the Paradoxical Depths

role of the digital. The revival in the past 20-30 years, which McCorkle calls appropriately "our present time," has focused largely on the design and dissemination of both print and digital documents. McCorkle explains that rehabilitations of the canon in the past 20-30 years have focused on "making it theoretically relevant to the realm of written discourse, as well as newly emerging modes of textual production combining multiple media forms" (29).

One of the first sources that McCorkle cites is John Frederick Reynolds's edited collection, *Rhetorical Memory and Delivery: Classical Concepts for Contemporary Composition and Communication*. McCorkle explains that chapters by Kathleen Welch, Jay David Bolter, Robert Connors, and Sam Dragga contribute to the view that delivery should assume concerns with written delivery, namely document design, presentation, and the media through which they are disseminated. McCorkle also cites communication scholar Laura J. Gurak's book, *Persuasion and Privacy in Cyberspace: The Online Protests Over Lotus MarketPlace and the Clipper Chip*. Gurak explores the ways in which "the shape of activist discourse" is predicated on the medium in which it occurs, and the ways in which electronic media are associated with delivery. Finally, McCorkle cites Kathleen Welch's scholarship because it is "perhaps the most persistent and influential scholar working to redefine delivery" (35). Influenced by Marshall McLuhan's approach to media and Walter Ong's theory of secondary orality, Welch calls for a revitalization of delivery and medium. In her contribution to the above-mentioned collection by Reynolds, Welch argues, "If delivery is regarded as medium, then the dynamics of the canon are reinvested with their original power" (Reynolds 99).

In addition to McCorkle's study is Jim Ridolfo and Danielle Nicole DeVoss's webtext, "Composing for Recomposition: Rhetorical Velocity and Delivery," in which they offer a brief overview of recent works associated with delivery. In addition to several sources that McCorkle cited, too, they highlight the work of John Trimbur, Danielle Nicole DeVoss and James Porter, Doug Eyman, and Virginia Skinner-Linnenberg. All of these scholars offer redefinitions of the canon, extending its scope to include design, presentation, medium as well as the method of production. Except for Skinner-Linnenberg, whose pedagogical focus retains a focus on bodies, the other contributions oftentimes eschew the body in order to focus on delivery and its associations with writing.

As innovative as these revisions of the canon are, the body has not benefited much from them. In order to revive the body, it is essential that rhetoric scholarship move beyond the long, traditional distrust that is implied by the consistent call to regulate, master, and otherwise limit its role. One way forward is to redefine the body as an ethological milieu along which

Suasive Iterations

its creative potentials are spread out and across other bodies, such as are found in the novel space-times of an immersive computing environment in which eversion can serve new, suasive ends.

My call to redefine the body as an ethological milieu is based on philosopher Gilles Deleuze's essay, "Spinoza and Us." In that essay, Deleuze challenges his readers to both redefine what a body is and how to value it. His challenges are inspired by the early modern philosophy of Baruch Spinoza. Deleuze begins with a definition of the body that resembles a two-dimensional vector space. He defines the two dimensions of a body in terms of its speeds and affective capacities:

> A body, of whatever kind, is defined by Spinoza in two simultaneous ways. In the first place, a body, however small it may be, is composed of an infinite number of particles; it is the relations of motion and rest, of speeds and slownesses between particles, that define a body, the individuality of a body. Secondly, a body affects other bodies, or is affected by other bodies; it is this capacity for affecting and being affected that also defines a body in its individuality. These two propositions appear to be very simple; one is kinetic and the other, dynamic. (123)

Deleuze elaborates on this definition in several ways. First, he expands the ways in which these two dimensions can be understood. Of the first, the "kinetic proposition," Deleuze explains that a focus on "relations of speeds and slownesses" implies that a body is not defined by its forms or functions. Deleuze writes, "The important thing is to understand life, each living individuality, not as a form, or a development of form, but as a complex relation between differential velocities, between deceleration and acceleration of particles" (123).

Of the second definition of a body, the dynamic proposition, Deleuze explains that we do not define a body in terms of its form, functions, or organs; rather, we focus on its capacity for affecting and being affected" (123). Deleuze explains that a constant in Spinoza's approach to the body is to map the "maximum threshold and minimum threshold" of a body (124). It is an approach that should not seem that alien to a rhetorician. As an approach to change, rhetoric has traditionally used the body of language, which is intertwined on innumerable levels of speed, slowness, and affective capacity, with the thoughts and feelings of an audience, to produce a change, a new relation with other bodies.

In the second half of his essay, Deleuze associates the Spinozist approach to the body with ethology, a zoological approach to the study of animals in their natural habitats. Spinoza's concept of the body is inextricably

Plumbing the Paradoxical Depths

linked to Nature; likewise, an ethologist studies how individual animals are defined by their relations in and with nature. Deleuze also associates the two dimensions of Spinoza's concept with the geographical terms of latitude and longitude.

Taken together, the Spinozist-Deleuzian approach to the body radically redefines how the canon of digital delivery can be pursued in NUI environments such as the Kinect's. The rhetorical goal of delivery can now be transformed into an ethological engagement with the amplitudes of a body affected by an everted experience in an immersive computing environment. One or more bodies engage with the computationally defined space-time of the immersive environment, and new "affective amplitudes" can be designed. The suasive goal of rhetoric in a Kinect-based NUI environment is geared toward opening up new ways in which a body can be expressed along both dimensions of the Spinozist-Deleuzian vector space. Related to this, the canon of digital delivery would take on the inventional role of identifying new species of ethological bodies derived from the processes of transduction, allegorization, and eversion.

NUI and the *Kinect*

Now we stand at the brink of another potential evolution in computing. Natural-user interfaces (NUIs) seem to be in a position similar to the GUI in the early 1980s. (Wigdor and Wixon 5)

Natural-user interfaces, or NUIs, comprise a wide range of human-computer technologies including voice, touch, gesture, and stylus or pen. Examples of them abound today. Albeit with some ambivalence from the public, voice-activated telephone systems have been in operation since the 1990s, and voice-activated computing for the visually impaired has been available since the 1970s. Single and multi-touch technologies have been around for over forty years, and they are a ubiquitous part of our consumer landscape, from ATM machines to interactive kiosks in museums. Gestural interfaces are newer, but the use of swipes and various other forms of finger movements across screens have been around for decades.

As a computational paradigm, NUI has been touted as the third inflection point in popular computing. The first was the command-line interface (CLI), the second, the graphical user interface (GUI). So, while a fairly wide range of NUI technologies have been around for several or more decades, the recent successes of Apple's iPhone and iPad and Microsoft's Kinect (and their earlier Surface table) have led to a conspicuous rise in industry evangelism about gestural and multi-touch technologies—a lot of the hype coming from Microsoft employees past and present.

Suasive Iterations

In addition to the epigraph to this section, in which Wigdor and Wixon claim that NUI is replacing GUI, the following three statements emphasize the impact that the shift will have. The first is from Chief Research and Strategy Officer at Microsoft Craig Mundie, in an interview on Microsoft's news site: "The transition to a natural user interface will change everything from the way students write term papers and play computer games to how scientists study global population growth and its impact on our natural resources" ("Computing, Naturally"). The next one is from Bill Gates, who in the following excerpt from "The Power of the Natural User Interface," focuses his attention on Microsoft's Kinect:

> One of the most important current trends in digital technology is the emergence of natural user interface, or NUI. We've had things like touch screen and voice recognition for a while now. But with Kinect, we are seeing the impact when people can interact with technology in the same ways that they interact with each other. (Gates)

The third piece of industry evangelizing is from August de los Reyes. During and since his tenure at Microsoft, he has extolled the virtues of NUI in numerous interviews and presentations. In one presentation in particular titled "Predicting the Past," given while he was "Experience Architect" on Microsoft's Surface team, he offers a more detailed, socio-economic context for the value of NUI. Beginning with a reference to Johan Huizinga's book, *Homo Ludens: A Study of the Play Element in Culture*, De los Reyes argues that that we are experiencing a return of "homo ludens," and the rising importance of NUI technologies are both an expression of it and a symbol of its value (De los Reyes).

In his book, Huizinga argues that play is a central and generative aspect of culture. It both precedes and extends beyond the human context to include, for example, animal play. For Huizinga, play and culture are intertwined and expressive of a "twin union," but culture is not the culmination of the former; rather, play is the generative dimension and the basis of who we are and what we do. But in the 1930s, when Huizinga's book was published, he was far less optimistic about the future role of play in western society—especially in comparison to De los Reyes. According to Huizinga, there had been a marked decline in the importance of play in human cultures and society since the eighteenth century: "More and more the sad conclusion forces itself upon us that the play-element in culture has been on the wane ever since the eighteenth century, when it was in full flower" (206). Compared to the nineteenth and early twentieth centuries, the eighteenth century was an era of ludic expression unparalled in the West. An engagement with life in philosophy, rhetoric, politics, literature, art, music, and

Plumbing the Paradoxical Depths

dress was infused with play elements. But by the end of that century, the role of play had started to wane. Across Europe and the United States, as Westerners donned boilersuits in order to participate in the beginnings of an emergent industrial age, the four interrelated activities and concepts of work, production, rationalism, and utilitarianism squelched the playfulness of the preceding age. In the modernizing and industrializing west, play was marginalized and all but lost.

But over seventy years separate Huizinga's sadness from the optimism expressed in De Los Reyes's presentation. During that time, dramatic and well-documented changes have occurred in culture, communication, economy, and society. Compared to the first decades of the twentieth century in the United States, during which Taylorist and Fordist principles of rationalized work and life reigned—the apogee of European works by thinkers such as Ure and Babbage (Harvey 126)—the first decades of the twenty-first seem outright ludic. Even since the 1970s, when a burgeoning information age would replace early twentieth century brawn for the late twentieth century brains of the knowledge worker, in the early decades of the twenty-first century, emotions, empathy, and inventiveness have become the new cornerstones of what Daniel H. Pink calls a "conceptual age" in which *homo sapiens* gives way to *homo ludens*. In his book, *A Whole New Mind*, which De los Reyes cites in his presentation, Pink claims, "The future belongs to a very different kind of person with a very different kind of mind—creators and empathizers, pattern recognizers, and meaning makers" (1). Among the types of people contributing to this future are "artists, inventors, designers, storytellers, caregivers, consolers, and big picture thinkers" (1). Due to the three As—abundance, automation, and Asia—Pink claims that the rationalism and what might be called logocentrism of the Druckerian knowledge worker has been eclipsed by new forms of thinking that are infused with emotion and empathy: "We are moving from an economy and a society built on the logical, linear, computer-like capabilities of the Information Age to an economy and a society built on the inventive, empathetic, big-picture capabilities" (2). The conceptual age is one in which play is one of the "six senses." The six senses are meant to complement the "L-Directed" reasoning epitomized during the information age. Functional thinking must be augmented by a feel for design and aesthetics. The ability to reason and argue must be augmented by the ability to narrate, or tell stories. The value of increasingly specialized thought should be balanced by an ability to see the bigger picture, and to make connections. Empathetic reasoning—the ability to "forge relationships" with others—must be valued more fully. Seriousness must be balanced by the ability to laugh and play: "In the Conceptual Age, in work and in life, we all need to play" (66).

De los Reyes cites Pink's book because the focus on play resonates with his argument about NUI technologies. For De los Reyes, NUI technologies will be paradigm shifting because of the deep and significant dimension of play that designers and programmers can build in to NUI. And the reason that playfulness is a cornerstone of the future success of NUI is that it is a proven method of designing an emotional bond between a user and programmed behavior. For digital rhetoricians, De los Reyes's arguments underscore the power of NUI to engage in creative and rhetorically-powerful ways with the "structures of feeling" that define our emotional bonds in a given rhetorical context. It is an opportunity to redefine rhetorical delivery as an inventional platform for exploring new "affective amplitudes." Delivery is redefined as the ability to deliver to a body a new, everted experience of self and world.

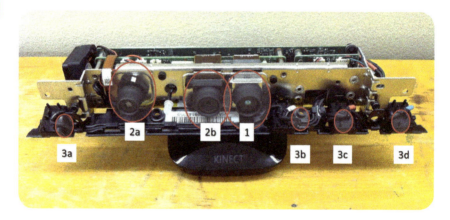

Figure 40. Partial teardown of the Kinect with key components numbered

The following technical review will allow us to more fully appreciate how the Kinect works as a transductive technology. Figure 40 is a partially torn-down of the Kinect sensor. The plastic covers that encase the electronic components have been removed, and labels have been added to the image to help define the position of the many parts in the sensor.

The most important parts of the Kinect are labeled 1, 2a, and 2b. These three technologies are the basis for the combined depth-sensing capabilities of the Kinect and the sensor's ability to detect and track human figures in its viewing area. Label 1 is a standard RGB camera. Label 2a is a Class A laser that emits a patterned grid of near-infrared "dots" in a cone-like spread in front of the sensor. Figure 41 below is an image of the dots taken with an infrared camera. While those "dots" cannot be detected by the human eye, they can be detected by an infrared camera (Label 2b). The

Plumbing the Paradoxical Depths

infrared camera on the original Kinect is a 640x480 camera. Based on the deformation of the "dots" in the patterned grid, the "time-of-flight" at which the "dots" bounce back from an object in front of the sensor, and specific information from the RGB camera's view, an onboard chip can detect and track as many as five different human figures within its viewing area, streaming the "joint" related data for the two active participants at 30 frames per second.

Depth-sensing cameras have been available for decades. Although there are a number of technological approaches, most of them (including the Kinect) use "time-of-flight" as a basis for defining depth or distance. The speed at which light bounces back from an object in the sensors field is translated spatially as a depth or distance. The longer it takes for a "dot" from the laser to bounce back, the farther away is the object.

The laser and camera (2a, b) are an essential part of the two data streams with which to experiment. The first is the "raw" depth data; the second is joint data associated with the human figures detected and tracked by the onboard chip.

Figure 41. Patterned dots from the Kinect captured with an infrared camera

The "raw" depth data streaming from the Kinect is sent as an array of 307,200 numerical values, at 30 frames-per-second (FPS). Although the 307,200 values are "packaged" as a single-dimensional, flattened-out list of numbers, they represent a two-dimensional, 640x480 snapshot of the scene in front of the sensor (307,200 = 640 x 480). The skeletal data

Suasive Iterations

streaming from the Kinect sensor is structured differently. Since the project in Chapter 4.5 is based on the raw depth data stream, the following explanation is brief. Skeletal data, which represents x-y-z data for each of twenty joints requires a unique data object type. At 30 FPS, the Kinect sends x-y-z data for as many as twenty joints for as many as two human figures (i.e., participants or players) detected by the system. An additional three figures can be tracked with less precision. When the Kinect detects a human figure, it assigns that figure a number and then breaks down the figure in to a series of 3D points which correspond to the twenty joints depicted in Figure 42.

In addition to the raw depth and skeletal data streams, which rely on the laser (Figure 40, label 1), and the two cameras (Figure 40, labels 2a, b), the Kinect also streams audio. Four downward-facing microphones (Figure 40, labels 3a-d) constitute an array that offers locative data about the audio picked up by the microphones. The locative properties of the audio data make it possible for a programmer to filter out speech that is not associated with a tracked figure in front of the sensor. The last of the sensors is an accelerometer.

Returning to the raw depth data streaming from the Kinect, the challenging and inspiring aspect of the stream is its pure potential. Like a pile of sand to which over nine million more grains are added each second and more than a half billion each minute, there is a potentially infinite number of ways in which to transduce their raw value. They can be subdivided into a series of smaller piles, or some of the grains can be sifted and removed. The sand can be melted or mixed with other materials ultimately to create new types of bodies. Since these grains are numerical, any number of mathematical operations can be performed on them, thereby transducing them toward new ends. Working with this experimental dune of data is challenging because of the seemingly infinite ways in which it can be molded or transduced. For all intents and purposes, raw depth is paradoxically flat.

Plumbing the Paradoxical Depths

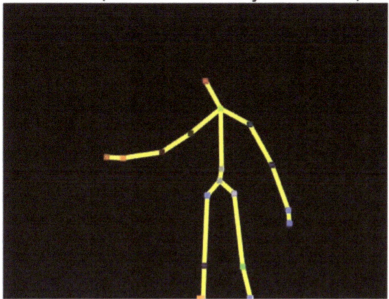

Figure 42. Skeletal joints identified by Kinect

Suasive Iterations

Manuel DeLanda is credited with developing the concept of a flat ontology. In *Intensive Science and Virtual Philosophy*, he introduces and expounds on its values. In the following excerpt, he introduces it in comparative terms:

> while an ontology based on relations between general types and particular instances is hierarchical each level representing a different ontological category (organism, species, genera), an approach in terms of interacting parts and emergent wholes leads to a flat ontology, one made exclusively of unique, singular individuals, differing in spatio-temporal scale but not in ontological status. (47)

Throughout his book, and especially in relation to this notion of flatness, DeLanda is challenging his readers to move beyond the divisible, hierarchically defined reality in which most scholars and artists spend their time. Inspired by Deleuze, who reconceptualizes the conventionally real world as an ever-changing actualization of intensive, virtual forces, DeLanda asks us to value life as something akin to a dune; Deleuze would call it a "body without organs."

To work with the raw depth data is to engage ontologically with a world in which subjects and objects are undifferentiated, in which depth-as-number is transformed into a radically transduce-able, intensive force. It is to work in a space-time in which participants have slipped below the surface of conventional meaning and perspective. From within the raw depth data, participants do not exist. They are immersed and distributed along a space-time in which their position and movements cannot be generalized, their types recast.

In his essay titled, "Paradoxical Bodies," José Gil reconceptualizes the movements and body of dancers in ways that reflect the flat ontology about which DeLanda writes as well as of the ethology of the body about which Deleuze wrote. In the following excerpt, DeLanda introduces his approach to the dancer's body:

> Here, we would like to consider the body no longer as a "phenomenon," no longer as a visible and concrete perception moving in the objective Cartesian space, but rather, we would like to consider the body as a meta-phenomenon, simultaneously visible and virtual, a cluster of forces, a transformer of space and time, both emitter of signs and trans-semiotic, endowed by an organic interior ready to be dissolved as soon as it reaches the surface. (Gil 94)

Gil's approach to the body is flat in the sense that it is one in which the conventional line between self and world are radically blurred. It implies

Plumbing the Paradoxical Depths

the ethological approach advocated by Deleuze, in which the issue is one of affective capacity. Especially for the dancer, who, with each newly inscribed gesture on his or her body, redefines what that body is in spatio-temporal terms, embodied movement is a flow without beginning or end.

This is the kind of body with which the Kinect's raw depth data allows digital rhetoricians to experiment. It is the kind of body that can lead to new ways of practicing and theorizing a body-centric canon of digital delivery. Transductive experimentations with the raw depth data can lead to strange, paradoxical happenings. With this sensor, we have the chance to suade bodies toward strange and everted space-times. There are momentary glimmerings of a strange, paradoxical relation in emBody(Text){, as individuals gather together and share an experience together as one. Just as in Rosenfield's descriptions of epideictic, there are moments when the work allows its participants to celebrate a slightly new and everted reality with each other, which they deliver to themselves.

4.5 The Paradoxical Depths of Delivery

In a dark, windowless room sits a first generation Kinect. There is a screen looming over participants stretching from floor to ceiling that plays a constantly changing multimodal composition. There is a surround sound system. A software program transduces the positions and movements of participants in the space in such a way as to allegorize them toward the kind of paradoxical relation about which Gil wrote. If participants are immersed in a compelling experience—if they are suaded by the eversion—there is a chance that they will be moved, rhetorically.

The first and second stages in the process of inventing a project like this are to develop a basic, technical understanding of the data's structure, and then to determine the analog/digital ranges with which you will be working. In Chapter 4, I stated that the Kinect's depth data is structured as an array of 307,200 numerical values, and that it is updated thirty times each second. Adding to that description, each of the 307,200 values represents a distance in meters from the sensor. Depth values are based on a range of approx. 0.4 to 5.3 meters away from the sensor, and the values in the array are negative floating-point values (-0.4000000 to -5.3000000). A value of 0.0 means that a distance at that corresponding point in the array couldn't be determined, which could mean that an object is out of range.

Although the 307,200 values comprise a single-dimensional array, it is relatively easy to reconstitute a two-dimensional image from it. This is because each 640-number segment of values in the array represents a row in the two-dimensional image, and the order of the 640-long segments corresponds to the "vertical" order of the scene, from top to bottom. If you want to reconstitute a two-dimensional image of the depths in a scene, you stack each of the 640-segment depth values one below the next with a couple of *for* loops or some other iterative function. Figure 43 is an illustration of the relationship between the array and the two-dimensional image.

It is important to note that the depth data is not a visual representation of the scene; so, if you want to visualize the depth-based scene in front of the Kinect, you need to transduce the metric values. The visualization in Figure 44 is based on Processing's map() method, which is used to transduce each floating point value to one of the 256 shades of gray.

The Paradoxical Depths of Delivery

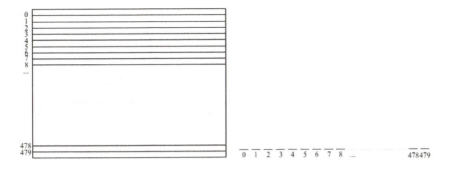

Figure 43. Illustration of structure of 2-D and 1-D depth data.

Figure 44. Gray-scale visualization of Kinect's depth data stream.

The larger the depth value, the lighter the shade of gray. In other words, a value of -1.3000000 (1 1/3 meters from the sensor), will be shaded lighter than -3.0000000 (3 meters from the sensor). This simple visualization of the depth data can be associated with the second stage in the inventional process.

In Chapter 4, I also explained that the rhetorical moment associated with the Kinect's raw depth data emerges along the line of eversion that a digital rhetor develops. A way of understanding this line of eversion is to associate it with what Anna Munster has called an extensive vector. In her book, *Materializing New Media*, Munster points to the dynamic on which I am focused when she writes the following:

> Computers offer us multiplications and extensions of our bodily actions... These multiplications by no means provide seamless matches between body and code; the mismatch characteristics of divergent series triggers the extension of our corporeality out toward our informatic counterparts... It is this extensive vector that draws embodiment away from its historical capture within a notion that the body is a bounded interiority. (33)

As the extensive vector about which Munster writes is augmented (stylistic hyperbole) in novel, stylistic ways, digital rhetoricians have the opportunity to develop new, paradoxical bodies expressive of hybridized structures of feeling. The mismatch about which Munster writes is a basis for eversion, based on an allegorization of bodies-as-code.

Moving on to stage three, if we begin with an individual data point or pixel within the 640x480 depth image, our list of events, actions, and ambient changes might begin with whether an object or person occupies the space that a single data point represents. If an object or person is in the field of vision, the list could include its position from the sensor as well as whether the value of the data point is changing:

> Single data point
>> Object/person in field of vision
>>> Position in front of sensor
>>> Static or moving
>>>> Forward or back
>> Object/person outside field of vision

But a more sophisticated approach to stage three would begin with a restructuring of the data. (Arguably, this could be characterized as a return to stage two, but I will continue as if restructuring the data is associated with the third). The first step toward a restructuring of the data begins with the realization that the array of depth values, i.e., the three-dimensional space in front of the sensor, can be rearranged or sub-divided into any number of configurations. The data can be recomposed as a series of contiguous cuboids, a set of concentric circles, or any other series of interrelated shapes. When we score up the relatively smooth and continuous space in front of the Kinect, we have transduced the data in a way that lends itself to even more sophisticated forms of transduction.

The Paradoxical Depths of Delivery

As an homage to the era of hypertext, the following approach to restructuring the data is based on a 4x4 grid; it is also a relatively easy way to score up the space. My idea is that the space in front of the Kinect can be divided among sixteen regions, and each region can act like a link in a hypertextual system. When one or more participants stand or move around in front of the Kinect, they activate one or more regions within the 4x4 structure. As one or more participants move through the sixteen-region space, their transduced movements can be allegorized toward a suasive end.

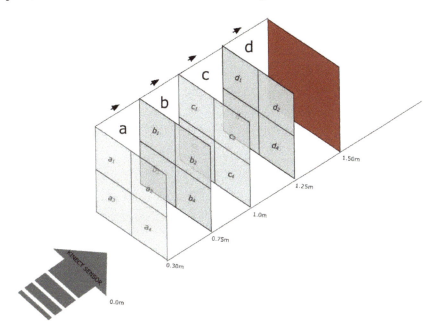

Figure 45. Illustration of 'transductive interface' for *Kinect*-based experimentation with depth data.

The visualization dashboard in Figure 46 includes depictions of the regions. Each region is numbered. In the illustration, the participant in front of the sensor is occupying region 5. As she moves, the number of the active region will change. For all intents and purposes, the structure is an abstract, stylistic platform for transductive invention.

Based on a 4x4 grid, the list for stage three can be revised as follows:

Data grid (4x4 grid)
    If the space in front of the Kinect is active (-.4 - -5.3 data values)

Suasive Iterations

> Participants are not moving
>> Number of active region/s
>> Duration region is active
> Participants are moving
>> Moving slowly or quickly among regions
>> Moving toward the left or right
>> Moving toward or away from the sensor
>> Moving diagonally
> If the space in front of the Kinect is not active (0.0 data values)
>> Last active region
>> Duration space is inactive

The list of actions and events associated with the restructured data is the basis for the next stage, allegorization.

The inventional goal of stage four is to develop a list of the ways in which participatory engagements with the sixteen-region grid of data can be allegorized. In other words, how can actions or events identified in stage three, such as moving toward the left or right and moving diagonally, be allegorized? To begin with, since the sixteen-region space is supposed to represent a hypertextual grid, the list from stage three could be paired with well-documented styles of linking, such as those "botanized" by Mark Bernstein. In his essay, "Patterns of Hypertext" Bernstein offers his readers an annotated taxonomy of hypertextual linking styles. One of the patterns that he lists is called the Counterpoint, which he describes as follows:

> In Counterpoint, two voices alternate, interleaving themes or welding together theme and response. Counterpoint often gives a clear sense of structure, a resonance of call and response reminiscent at once of liturgy and of casual dialogue. (Bernstein).

Casuistically stretching Bernstein's description of counterpoint to the transduced, computational space in front of the Kinect, an allegorized version of it might be based on a dynamic between two (or more) active regions. In other words, if two or more participants activate two or more regions in the sixteen-region space, their positions could be associated with a counterpoint. Their actions could then be folded together, and their movements could be the basis for the screenic and sonic feedback that immerses them in the space.

Stage five in the inventional process culminates in the creation of a visualization dashboard. Figure 46 is a screenshot of a dashboard developed for the 4x4 grid.

The Paradoxical Depths of Delivery

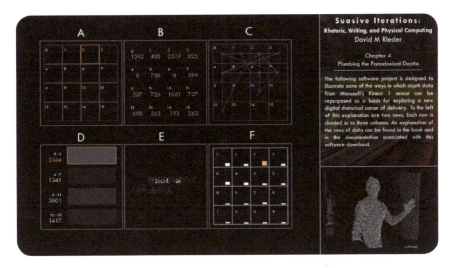

Figure 46. Visualization dashboard of depth data for transductive experimentation.

Figure 46 is one possible contribution to the inventional process. It is a visualization dashboard for transductive experiments with the Kinect's depth data. This dashboard is just one possible way in which to begin experimenting with the data stream.

In the bottom-right corner of the dashboard is the gray-scale visualization of the two-dimensional depth data image from stage two. It is there as a point of reference. On the left side of the visualization are six data explorations labeled A-F. They are all based on the sixteen cuboid regions. The first row of visualizations labeled A-C are related to each other. In the box labeled A, an overhead view of the 4x4 rectangular cuboid is visualized; in Box D, an alternative and simpler overhead is on display of a 1x4 grid. The row with quadrants (Q) 0-3 is closest to the Kinect sensor; looking out from the sensor, Q0 and Q3 are the left and right quadrants, respectively. The Q within the 4x4 cuboid that has been identified as the most "active" or occupied is highlighted. In Figure 46, it is Q3. What this means is that the person in the visualization in the bottom-right corner of the dashboard is in the row closest to the sensor and left of center.

The basis for identifying the most active region in the 4x4 grid is displayed in Box B. Those numbers are based on an evaluation of a sampling of the 307,200 depth values sent to Processing 30 times each second. Since there's no reason to evaluate every one of the 307,200, the loop only evaluates every fourth value, or 76,800 values total. Lowering the resolution of the evaluation saves processing power for other computational goals. Each space in the 4x4 grid is based on a minimum and maximum depth range as well as on its position along the X-axis of the implied 640x480 image. When one of the 76,800 values is sampled, and its value is not 0.0, it is recorded as an active pixel within one of the sixteen spaces. The space with the highest number of active pixels is the most active space. In Boxes A and B, that space is Q2 with 2519 active pixels. If we were developing this visualization with Bernstein's counterpoint in mind, we could rewrite the Processing code in order to highlight the two most active regions.

Boxes C and F imply one possible way in which to develop a paradoxical, everted experience. As the software program runs, a history of the regions that have been activated is recorded, and a line is drawn from one region in Box C to the next. In Box F below it, a recording of the number of times each region has been activated is presented. Based on the data collected by Boxes C and F, it would be possible to identify patterns of activation that coincide with one or more of the hypertextual patterns in Bernstein's essay. If those patterns are unknown to the participants in the space, an eversion of their personal sense of agency could give way to the realization that the algorithm tracking and transducing their positions and movements is the agent of change. As two or more participants realize that their combined activities within the space are secondary to an algorithm, they may begin to act as one, participating in a kind of shared agency that becomes paradoxical in the sense described by Gil.

Box E is a simple example of the way in which the opacity and position of a few words on a screen can be transformed based on a hypertextual transduction of the 4x4 grid of depth data. If we replace Box E with a large screen and surround sound system, participants could lose themselves in an exploration of a hypertextual narrative which they can't directly control. A loss of control could be the first step toward the establishment of a paradoxical body comprising two or more participants and an algorithm that is waiting for the right combination of active regions to allegorize their combined efforts toward the next transduction of text, image, and sound. Revising the visualization dashboard in order to fully explore the hypertextual possibilities of the project would be an ongoing process of inventional work.

5 A Call for Distant (Transductive) Writing

*'Distant reading,' I have once called this type of approach; where distance is however not
an obstacle, but a specific form of knowledge: fewer elements, hence a sharper sense of their
overall interconnection. Shapes, relations, structures. Forms. Models.*

— Franco Moretti, *Graphs, Maps, Trees*

Inspired in part by Franco Moretti's term, "distant reading," this chapter
is an argument for the establishment of *distant* writing practices. But let
me be clear about a few things. First, I am not advocating that digital writers
adopt the "big data" computational practices on which Moretti relies. In
fact, I am not advocating that we focus on analytics at all; rather, distant
writing is related to invention and rhetorical appeal. Nor am I going to
claim that distant writing operates under the auspices of digital humanities.
Any one of those approaches could be a productive pathway for writing, but
they are not the ones to which this chapter is devoted.

What I find inspiring about Moretti's call for distant reading is related to the way it challenges literary scholars to rethink their long-standing
reliance on close reading strategies. In an era of Google Books and digital
libraries like the Hathi Trust, which host millions of digitized novels, essays, poems, transcribed speeches, and other textual artifacts, the persistent
practice of the close reading misses the digital forest for the textual trees.
An individual scholar—even a team—cannot possibly "hand" read a literary
corpus comprising thousands, hundreds of thousands, or millions of texts.
Close reading strategies are the wrong scale for scholarly research in the
information age. According to Moretti, a computational approach is the
correct scale. While it operates at a remove from any one individual text,
the distance at which it works can lead to the discovery of large-scale textual
patterns that would be inaccessible under closer scrutiny. Distance is a new
albeit paradoxical form of closeness in an increasingly digitized era of scholarship and reading.

As a writer in a digital age, the reason I find Moretti's approach
inspiring is the following: the persistent and conventional assumption that
writing is defined by its proximity (read: closeness) to speech and phonetic
thought is in need of a corresponding "rethink." Whereas distant reading
operates at a remove from individual texts, distant writing operates at a remove from speech and phonetic thought. Distant writing can be practiced in
any number of ways. In this chapter, it is a return to its origins in line-making practices that include tracing, drawing, etching, and more. The reasons
are two. First, line-making practices, such as those associated with circuit

Suasive Iterations

design, are an essential part of the transductive process in an era of physical computing. Second, NUI-based interfaces, which include touch and hands-free gesturing, can be broadly understood as multi-dimensional surfaces on which are written post-alphabetic lines.

Figure 47 is a circuit design developed in *Fritzing*, which is an open-source software program for drawing, documenting, and sharing the circuit designs on which a physical computing project is based. The colored lines in the circuit diagram are the wires that will be used to write electricity across the various components. In that diagram, there are four actuators to which electricity would be written to turn them on or off—two LEDs, a speaker, and a DC motor. There is also one sensor, a "force sensitive resistor," which can be used as an alternative to a pushbutton.

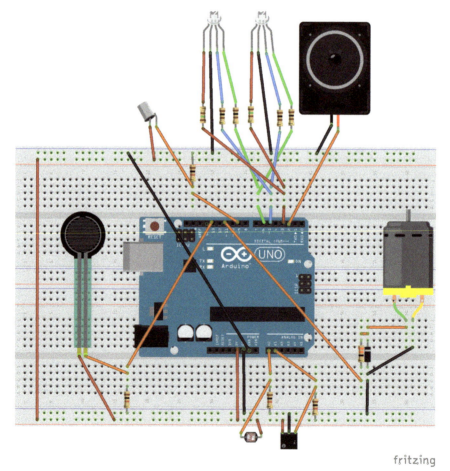

Figure 47. Fritzing circuit diagram of the IPlush project. Photo credit: Natalia Fargasch Norman.

A Call for Distant (Transductive) Writing

Many of the wires have transistors and other micro-components restricting the flow of electricity, in order to define a circuit that conforms to the limits of current associated with each part of the project. Except for a few words written on the microcontroller, and English-based code language in the software that transduces the analog data to and from the sensors and actuators, alphabetic writing has a marginal presence.

So long as we hold tight to a limited view of writing-as-alphabetic, we miss out on the opportunity to engage as writers in a broader, transductive process. Arguably, this is one of the implicit reasons that digital humanists like Moretti have distanced themselves from close reading. For Moretti, cutting-edge reading practices begin with digitized texts that have been prepared for numerate work environments. The text mining algorithms that Moretti and other digital humanists apply to the hundreds, thousands, even millions of texts rely on the fact that the texts that they process conform to Lev Manovich's first principle of new media, "Numerical Representation" (Manovich 27). Many of these texts may still be readable in the conventional sense, but their new value is numerate, not literate.

For digital writers, there's a lesson to be learned here, which is that we will find ourselves increasingly boxed out of cutting-edge work if we do not expand our definition of writing beyond the print-centric, alphabetic tradition. For distant writers, writing did not begin as a technology for representing speech, and there is no reason to think that it must be limited to that species of line-making practices in the future.

In the remainder of this chapter, I present arguments by Roy Harris and Tim Ingold in order to develop a theoretical framework for distant writing. Harris's contribution is critical: he provides distant writers with a way of "distancing" themselves from what he has called the "tyranny of the alphabetic," in order to explore new forms of writing, including what I would call the transductive. Ingold's contribution, by contrast, offers distant writers a genealogy of lines from which a general theory of writing can be built up. Together, Harris and Ingold provide distant writers with a theoretical basis for developing approaches to writing to which the alphabetic is a distant relative.

On the Line

Linguists like Harris are undervalued allies in the pursuit of writing studies "after the voice." Harris is interested in studying language unalloyed by the influences of literacy and "alphabetic" writing. The impact of writing and literacy on language needs to be acknowledged and then excised from the latter, if language is to be properly studied. To that end, a deep and thorough knowledge of writing's origins and influences are essential.

As it relates to distant writing, in his book, *The Origin of Writing*, Harris's contributions act like a wedge, opening up a space in which the historically and conceptually broader understanding of writing can be studied. For the purposes of this chapter, there are two ways in which he accomplishes this. First, he returns to the etymological origins of writing, which lead us to a much broader understanding of the term. Harris explains that the Ancient Greek and Egyptian words for writing were unrelated to the alphabetic legacy to which writing would be reduced in the early modern period. In Ancient Greek, the word γράφειν ("to write") originally meant to engrave, scratch, or scrape. In Ancient Egyptian, the same word was used for writing and drawing. According to Harris, this understanding of the term would persist into the sixteenth century (29). Criticizing the way in which historians ignored this broader definition of writing, Harris writes,

> The later restriction of such words to designate alphabetic writing hardly warrants the narrow perspective adopted by those historians of the subject who take for granted that graphic signs count as writing only when used for purposes which alphabetic writing was later to fulfill. (29-30)

Alphabetic writing is one possible approach to writing, and it was not the first. Before writing practices were reduced to representational support for language and speech, they were much more broadly defined.

The second way in which Harris drives a wedge between alphabetic and non-alphabetic forms of writing is to critique the accepted notion that writing represents speech. In the following excerpt, Harris states the problem to which his chapter is devoted:

> The question is whether alphabetic writing in its original or any of its traditional forms, was in fact designed to function as a system of "visible speech." Certainly it was and is used to record speech; but that is a different matter. . . . The doctrine that writing represents speech fudges the issue of exactly what represents what. (102)

This question is a provocative one for distant writers because it foregrounds the technological dimensions of writing. Yes, the core competency of alphabetic writing is to "record speech," but whether it represents speech is an entirely different issue—the uncritically accepted truth of which has been based on a series of misconceptions and misleading assumptions.

By the end of Harris's chapter, it becomes clear that what writing "represents" is not what we've been taught to believe and assume. Mid-way through his chapter, Harris foreshadows his conclusion, writing, "if there

A Call for Distant (Transductive) Writing

is any sense to be made of the thesis that writing represents speech, it is not the kind of sense which will afford the Aristotelian any comfort at all" (109). The Aristotelian theory to which Harris alludes is an important aspect of his conclusion because some of the misconceptions on which it is based persist. In *De Interpretatione*, Aristotle states, "Words spoken are symbols or signs of affections or impressions of the soul; written words are the signs of words spoken" (115). Harris explains that this Aristotelian theory will be echoed by Rousseau in the eighteenth century, and "by the twentieth [have] become no longer one possible view but an 'accepted fact'" (26). Citing the definition of writing in the eleventh edition of *Encyclopedia Britannica*, Aristotle's theory is echoed as follows: "the use of letters, symbols, or other conventional characters, for the recording by visible means of significant sounds" (Harris 26). And none other than Saussure will echo this theory when he characterizes language and writing as separate systems, and that the primary purpose of writing is to represent the former.

The Aristotelian theory, Harris explains, is predicated on what Harris calls "double symbolism" or "dual representation" (81). Dual symbolism is descriptive of the two-step process by which writing represents ideas: writing represents the sounds of the words uttered in speech, and speech represents the ideas (and soul) of the speaker. The letters of the alphabet are not interpretable—they do not represent an idea directly—but they do represent the individual sounds from which the words that do represent an idea are built.

Is it true that each of the letters of the alphabet represent the sounds of speech, that the words that we utter are built up from a sequence of separate and distinct sounds? Harris's answer is no: "The notion that each letter stands for one spoken segment involves an ideally simple correspondence" (90). So why would Ancient Greek thinkers as scrutinizing as Aristotle have accepted this theory? And why has it persisted to this day?

Harris offers two answers. The first is that it is expressive of Ancient Greek linguistic theory, and of the ways in which language related to "human perception, memory, and reality" (82). The second may seem somewhat curious, but as a parent who helped teach his children how to read and write, I find that it helps explain the persistent value of this theory of representation. Harris's "psychological" explanation of it begins with two forms of cat, the word and a drawing.

Harris introduces what I will call his "tale of two kats" as follows: "As children, we are taught that *c–a–t* is pronounced [kat] 'because' *c* stands for [k], *a* for [a], and *t* for [t], and 'because' the sequence [k] plus [a] plus [t] 'makes' [kat]" (88). But, Harris, asks, how would a child make sense of this "curious rationale"? (88). He proposes that s/he would rely on h/er experience "reading" another form of marks inscribed on paper, drawing. And the child would have already been taught that there is a difference between non-representational lines, such as scribbles and "pretty patterns," and pictures, which are representational. So, the letters, *c*, *a*, and *t*, are a "picture" of the spoken word [kat], and this picture correlates with the drawing of a cat. Harris concludes, "So there seems to be in the child's experience a ready-made answer to the question 'What are the letters drawings of'?" (89).

But what happens when the child is confronted with "silent" letters, which problematize the pedagogical lesson? Although the child will be taught that silent letters are merely exceptions, their silence is paradigmatic of the moment when the lesson starts to show its limits. Underscoring his point, Harris writes, "If we are taught to put 'silent' letter in spelling certain words, why are we not taught to put in 'silent' strokes when drawing the corresponding objects" (89). In the following excerpt, Harris offers a fictional scenario related to the silent *k* in the word, knot:

> The knot in your shoelace is spelled with a silent *k*; but can we imagine a system of drawing which demanded in the corresponding picture a visually superfluous loop or squiggle? ("You haven't drawn the shoelaces very well, darling. You forgot to put in the extra bit on the knot—remember, the bit that isn't there?"). (89)

Harris concludes his critique of the "psychological" reason for the persistence of Aristotle's mistaken theory of representation as follows: "Speaking, comprehension of speech, reading and writing are four extremely complex activities. Even though the Aristotelian theory is flawed, if it helps build confidence around such difficult learning tasks, it makes sense to continue with it." (90). But this "pedagogically inculcated illusion" should be challenged by distant writers, since it inadvertently limits the ways in which writing can be defined and subsequently practiced.

Supporting Harris's "psychological" or pedagogical basis for Aristotelian theory is Gunther Kress's study of children learning how to write. In *Before Writing: Rethinking the Paths to Literacy*, Kress documents the ways in which several children gradually acquire reading and writing skills. In the following passage, Kress echoes the psychological challenges that following the transition from drawing pictures to writing letters:

> [Children] make signs which are founded on a motivated relation between meaning and form, signified and signifier. That is the overriding principle with which they approach the world of alphabetic writing. And then they come up against the brick wall of a system

A Call for Distant (Transductive) Writing

which in a number of ways and at a number of levels resists an understanding in those terms. There's simply no reason, no "motivation",
for a shape such as E expressing the sound of e as in Emily. . . . At this
point, the child's logic does not work. (Kress 73)

Based on Kress's description, teaching children that alphabetic
characters represent the sounds of speech may be inaccurate, but it is a necessary pedagogical means to an end.

Returning to Harris, where does Aristotle's doctrine go wrong? In
the following quote, Harris offers his answer:

The answer is that it goes astray by misconstruing a complex of pedagogically inculcated practices as evidence of a representational relationship between writing and speech, while at the same time reserving
the right not to come clean on the twin questions of what represents
what, and how. We are expected to have an "intuitive" grasp of this
relationship, and not to question it. (108)

For distant writers, coming clean on the "twin questions" leads to
a more sophisticated understanding of both alphabetic writing and writing
more broadly construed. After all, if the letter *c* preceding the vowels *a*, *o*,
and *u* is pronounced [k], but is pronounced [s] when it precedes *e*, *i*, and *y*,
which, confusedly, overlaps with the sound of the letter *s*, what exactly does
the letter *c* represent? Its representational role is more complex than we
have been taught.

As we pry apart the presumed relationship between alphabetic writing and speech, an opportunity arises for distant writers to develop a more
sophisticated understanding of how the two are related, which can lead to an
appreciation of the broader range of practices to which the term "writing"
should be applied.

For distant writers, the conclusion to which I'm leading is that all
writing, including alphabetic writing, is a *transductive* technology. Alphabetic writing transduces the continuous, multi-dimensional, spatio-temporal
flow of sound associated with speech. Alternative, distant forms of writing
could be developed to transduce other sources of physical energy, such as
heat, light, touch, and movement.

The presumption that speech is composed of a sequential series of
discrete sounds is symptomatic of the legacy of the alphabet and especially
print-based writing. Speech is far more complex—and far less atomistic—
than the alphabet would have us believe. But it is the pedagogical legacy as
well as of the practices of reading and writing that contribute to this belief. For another linguist, Michael Studdert-Kennedy, whom Harris cites

Suasive Iterations

in support of his argument, speech is more like a continuous flow of sound. In the following excerpt from his essay titled "The Phoneme as Perceptuomotor Structure," Studdert-Kennedy counters the "atomistic" assumption about speech and presents a more complex and dynamic description of what speech is:

> We do not normally speak phoneme by phoneme, syllable by syllable, or even word by word. At any instant, our articulators are executing a complex interleaved pattern of movements of which the spatio-temporal coordinates reflect the influence of several neighboring segments. The typical result is that any isolable articulatory or acoustic segment arises as a vector of forces from more than one linguistic segment, while any particular linguistic segment distributes its forces over several articulatory and acoustic segments. (Studdert-Kennedy 68)

Studdert-Kennedy's description of the continuous, acoustic flow of speech reminds me of leaves picked up by the wind. Slowly making their way down the street as a swirling mass, the sibilance that attends them is expressive of the distribution of articulated force holding the mass together.

Echoing Studdert-Kennedy's description of the relationship between speech and writing is another linguist whom Harris cites. In his *Principles of the History of Language*, H. Paul writes, "[speech] is essentially a continuous series of infinitely numerous sounds, and alphabetical symbols do no more than bring out certain characteristic points of this series in an imperfect way" (Paul 39; Harris 114). Underscoring Paul's point, and alluding to the Zenoic paradox of discrete vs. continuous value, known as the "dichotomy paradox," Harris explains,

> In other words, there is no question of using a separate symbol for each sound because sounds are not discrete segmental units. Or if they are, there must be an infinite number of them in even the "shortest" spoken word: for the same reason that there is an infinite number of sequential divisions in an inch. (114).

What we learn from Paul, Studdert-Kennedy, and Harris is that alphabetic writing is not a representational technology—at least not in the ways in which we've been taught and have long-presumed since Aristotle. It's more like a transductive technology that captures some of the articulatory moments comprising the analog flow of speech.

For Harris in particular, the "tyranny of the alphabet" limits our appreciation of the complexity of speech *and* the alphabet, which inadvertently constrains us to a limited role for writing. When we problematize the conventional, representational definition of alphabetic writing, we have the opportunity to redefine alphabetic writing as a (relatively low-resolution) transductive mark-up language; and when that happens, we have the opportunity to think in far broader terms about the scope of our field.

Writing on the Line

Moving on from Harris, one of the thinkers who offers distant writers a broader view of writing is Tim Ingold. In *Lines: A Brief History*, Ingold has developed a cross-cultural exploration of line-making practices that include weaving, drawing, writing, and other, indirect forms of linear production, such as walking paths demarcated by trampled grass and animal footprints in the snow. Although Ingold doesn't offer any examples from microelectronics, lines are found throughout hardware and software design. In fact, working in physical computing introduces us to an entirely new experience of line-making in soldering and circuit design as well as in the new kinds of natural-user interfaces with which users interact. Extrapolating from his study of lines, Ingold offers distant writers a way of explaining how the lines and line-making practices associated with the new era of computing are conceptually related to the kinds of lines that we usually deploy in alphabetic and other forms of writing.

Ingold explains that his interest in a study of lines began with a question about the distinctions between speech and song. Until relatively recently in the West, music was a verbal art. Speech and song were inextricably linked. Citing a passage from *The Republic*, Ingold cites Socrates's definition of music as "composed of three things, the words, the harmony, and the rhythm" (6). Ingold explains, "The words, then, are not just an integral part of music; they are its leading part" (7). For the Ancient Greeks, music without words was little more than an embellishment or an accompaniment. The point of this Ancient Greek theory is that "Plato's rule" persisted until the end of the Middle Ages, when the rule would give way to nonverbal forms of music. In the following excerpt, Ingold dramatizes some of his thought process leading up to his focus on line-making:

> How can this come about? The search for an answer led me from mouth to hand, from vocal declamations to manual gestures, and to the relation between these gestures and the marks they leave on surfaces of all kinds. Could it be that the silencing of language had something to do with changes in the way writing itself is understood: as an art of verbal composition rather than manual inscription? My inquiry into line-making had begun. (1-2)

Ingold's first chapter begins with a focus on the modern silencing of language and the separation of words from music, and by the end of it, he's established precedent for a study of lines that includes writing among its species. The specific questions to which he is devoted is the following: "how did it come about that the essential musicality of song was transferred from its verbal to its non-verbal components of melody, harmony, and rhythm? And conversely, how was the sound taken out of language?" (8). Beginning with the first question, Ingold explains that this question piqued his interest because, for most of its history in the West, music had been a verbal art. Ingold writes, "The musical essence of song lay in the sonority of its words" (1). So when and why did music become wordless—or we might say voiceless? As Ingold researched this issue, he came across a second and complementary one, which he introduces as follows: "we have also arrived at a notion of language as a system of words and meanings that is given quite independently of its actual voicing in the sounds of speech" (1). His answers to these questions lead to his focus on lines.

As it relates to my proposed approach to distant writing, Ingold realized that the reason music became wordless and language silent was related to the impact of sophisticated notational practices in both fields. Beginning with music, Ingold offers a brief history of musical notation beginning with the *neuma* and ending with the modern stave score. What had been for centuries a supplement to the words, the value of which was mnemonic (to remind a singer about specific musical emphasis within a score), would eventually become a full-fledged form of notation from which a musician could perform a piece without ever having heard it before.

A "decisive step" toward what would become the modern stave score occurred in the eleventh century, when Guido d'Arezzo recommended broader changes to the long-standing neumes and punctuational marks. Based on his recommendations, "a man could learn to sing a verse without ever having heard it before" (Ingold 22). D'Arezzo's recommendations shortened the time that it took his students to learn to sing a melody. Centuries later, his changes to the ancient *neumes* and punctuational marks would be further transformed into a notational system fully independent of lyrics. When this happened, sound and word would be separated. The ability to sight read was born. Ingold concludes,

> Once music is cut loose from words, what had before been an indivisible, poetic unity, namely the song, became a composite of two things, words and sounds. Thenceforth the single register of song, written in letters and words but embellished with accents and inflections indicated by means of both *neumes* and punctational marks, was split into

A Call for Distant (Transductive) Writing

two distinct registers, one of language and the other of music, notated respectively by separate lines of script and score which were to be read in parallel. (23)

Why did music lose its voice? Because the notational system became sophisticated enough to forgo the use of words to convey the melody.

Turning to the silencing of language, Ingold begins with a brief point about Ferdinand de Saussure's theory of language, which is paradigmatic of the silenced perspective. From there, he turns to Walter Ong only to discover that Ong's "single axis of contrast" theory is based on an historical discrepancy.

Ingold begins with Ferdinand de Saussure's theory of language, which is exemplary of the modern silencing of language. He writes, "At first glance, Saussure seems as committed as his pre-modern forebears to the principle of the sonority of the word" (7). From Saussure's *Course in General Linguistics*, Ingold cites the claim that the only "true bond" is "the bound of sound" (7). But Ingold points out that "words, for Saussure, do not exist in their sounding" (8). Ingold continues, "Understood in a purely physical or material sense, therefore, sound cannot belong to language. It is, says Saussure, 'only a secondary thing, substance to be put to use.'" And he continues, "In language, then, there are no sounds as such; there are only what Saussure calls *images* of sound" (8). Ingold concludes that, for Saussure, sound is physical/material, but the "sound-image" is a psychological phenomenon. It exists as an "imprint" on the surface of the mind (8).

Ingold asks how Saussure's silencing of language might have occurred. He turns to Walter Ong for an answer. According to Ong, the silencing of language is due to the influence of the written word. Ingold summarizes Ong's position in the following excerpt:

Apprehending words as they are seen on paper, both motionless and open to prolonged inspection, we readily perceive them as objects with an existence and meaning quite apart from their sound in acts of speech. It is as though listening to speech were a species of vision—a kind of seeing with the ear, or "earsight"—in which to hear spoken words is akin to looking at them. (8-9)

Ingold follows up, asking whether it is possible that Saussure could have developed his idea of a "psychological imprint" without the influence of writing. Ong, Ingold relays, "thinks not."

Ong is not alone in his assessment of the influence of writing on speech—but that does not mean it is without controversy. Ingold for one goes on to argue against Ong. Considering the fact that music as a "verbal art" persisted throughout the Middle Ages, a discrepancy seems to exist in Ong's theory of writing's influence on speech. Ingold sets up a distinction between a pre-modern and modern experience of reading and writing that challenges the traditional narrative offered by Ong, who draws sharp distinctions between speech and writing. Ingold writes,

> If Ong is right to claim that the effect of writing is to establish language as a separate domain of words and meanings, detached from the sounds of speech, then the division between language and music would have been installed at the very origin of writing itself. (9)

Since this is not what occurred historically, there must be another way of theorizing the rise of silent language and non-verbal music.

	Notational	Non-notational
The work itself	SCRIPT	DRAWING
Work as class of compliant performances	SCORE	ETCHING

Figure 48. Ingold's Table of Non-/Notational Pratices.

Ingold's approach is based on the table in Figure 48. Compared to the conventional "single axis of contrast" that stretches between orality and literacy, on which Ong relies, Ingold posits two independent axes of contrast (see Figure 48). Ingold argues that the two axes lead to a more sophisticated understanding of change. The first axis of contrast is "aural and visual sensory modalities." The second is bodily gesture, which may include vocal, manual, or both forms, and the inscription of that bodily gesture as "a trace on some material surface" (27). These two axes lead to four alternatives, which Ingold enumerates as follows: "1) aural-gestural, 2) visual-inscriptional, 3) aural-inscriptional, and 4) visual-gestural" (27).

A Call for Distant (Transductive) Writing

According to Ingold, numbers 1 and 2 correspond to "our contemporary understandings of ordinary speech and writing respectively" (27). We assume generally that speech comprises "vocal gestures that are heard," and that writing comprises "inscribed traces that are seen" (27). The problem with this contemporary understanding is that it ignores the relationship between gestures and inscriptions. Ingold explains, "Thus, writing has been understood simply as a visual representation of verbal sound, rather than as the enduring trace of a dexterous manual movement" (27-28). For Ingold, the fourth alternative, the "visual apprehension of manual gesture," is the one that leads to a new theorization of both writing and music as well as to new way of understanding the moment when language lost its voice.

Ingold's introduction of the fourth "visual-gestural" alternative is provocative—especially when we associate it with his claim that a study of lines must include the surfaces with which they are associated. The reason, I contend, is that the surface associated with a line is an expression of the "enduring trace" of manual movement, or of a "post-human" set of forces.

For Ingold, print-based writing is disembodied and disconnected from the expressive force of the gesture, which is why it is possible for writing to be reduced to the second alternative. And while Ong and other scholars have promoted the idea that writing established language as a separate realm, leading to its silencing, Ingold claims that it is print-based writing (not hand writing) that is the culprit. In fact, the historical timeline is more easily reconciled when it is associated with a focus on print-based writing.

As it relates to the establishment of distant writing practices, Ingold's critiques of Saussure and Ong shake some of the established foundations of writing theory in and around composition studies. Saussure—but especially Ong—are influential theorists of language and writing in rhetoric and composition, and Ingold has highlighted the ways in which they reinforce a narrow, logocentric definition of writing. Distant writers must look outside of some of the established texts in writing studies to justify non-alphabetic work as writerly.

One final contribution from Ingold's book is his taxonomy of lines. Following his chapter on writing, speech, reading, and music, Ingold turns to the questions of surfaces. He explains their importance in the following excerpt:

> As I delved into the history of writing in the Western world, and especially the transition from the manuscript of medieval times to the modern printed text, it became clear that what was at stake was not merely the nature of the lines themselves, and of their production.

Suasive Iterations

Most of the lines in question were inscribed on parchment or paper. Yet the ways in which they were understood depended critically on whether the plain surface was compared to a landscape to be traveled or a space to be colonized, or to the skin of the body or the mirror of the mind. . . . For just as the history of writing belongs within the history of notation, and the history of notation within the history of the line, so there can be no history of the line that is not also about the changing relations between lines and surfaces. (39)

Based on the dynamic relationship between lines and surfaces, Ingold offers a comparative taxonomy of four "major classes" of lines: threads, traces, cuts (cracks and creases), and ghostly lines. A thread is "a filament of some kind." It can contribute to an entanglement or be "suspended between points in three dimensional space" (41). His list of examples is divided between human-made and natural. Of the former are "a ball of wool, a skein of yarn, a necklace, a cat's cradle . . . an electrical circuit, telephone lines, violin strings" (41). The latter include "roots, rhizomes, and fungal mycelia," "sprouts, stems, and shoots," the network of veins traversing leaves, coniferous needles, spider webs, and the "external hairs and feathers, antennae and whiskers, and [the] internal vascular and nervous systems" of mammals, birds, fish, and insects. The thread distinguishes itself from the second class of line, the trace, in that the former is not drawn on a surface. Compared to the thread, the trace "is any enduring mark left in or on a solid surface by a continuous movement" (43). Of traces, Ingold further distinguishes three sub-types. The first two are additive and subtractive traces. Handwriting and drawing are typically additive. Scratched, scored, or etched lines are subtractive. The third is harder to name, so Ingold offers an example. Citing artist Richard Long's work titled "A Line Made by Walking," which was created by pacing up and down a field until "a line appeared in the grass" (43), Ingold writes, "Though scarcely any material was removed by this activity, and none was added, the line shows up in the pattern of reflected light from countless stems of grass bent underfoot" (43).

Handwriting is usually associated with tracing, and Ingold expands on this relationship when he writes, "The word *writing* originally referred to the incisive trace-making of this kind" (43). Continuing, in the following excerpt, Ingold expands on the etymology of the word, writing, as well as of its connection to drawing:

In Old English the term *writan* carried the specific meaning "to incise runic letters in stone." Thus one would write a line by drawing a sharp point over a surface: the relation between drawing and writing is here

A Call for Distant (Transductive) Writing

between the gesture—of pulling or dragging the implement—and the line traced by it, rather than, as it is conventionally understood today, between lines of fundamentally different sense and meaning. (43)

Before moving on to the third class of line, Ingold writes, "Though I started out by presenting threads and traces as though they were categorically differentiated . . . In reality, each stands as a transform of the other. Threads may be transformed into traces, and traces into threads" (52). This will prove to be an especially important point as we return from a summary of Ingold's chapter to its implications for both Vitanza's "wayve" theory of writing and Sarah Arroyo's theory of the swipe.

The third class of line combines cuts, cracks, and creases, which is "created not by adding material to surfaces, or by scratching it away, but by ruptures in the surfaces themselves" (44). Citing Kadinsky's claim that a capacity of lines is to create surfaces, Ingold notes that some cuts can generate additional surfaces, such as when "a spade cuts the surface of the soil . . . creating a new, vertical surface of the soil" (45). Other cuts divide materials. Ingold cites the way in which the Saami people of Lapland cut the ears of reindeer into patterns. Ingold writes, "Saami people would traditionally describe each pattern as a word, and the cutting of the mark as an act of writing" (45). Cracks in a surface both distinguish themselves from cuts and associate themselves with the second class of lines because they can interrupt traces, which might then lead to the establishment of a thread across it: "in the landscape, a path of travel may be interrupted by a precipitous gorge in an otherwise level plateau. To get across, you have to construct a bridge, whereupon the trace becomes a thread" (45). Finally, there are creases, which include pleats and folds in various fabrics as well as wrinkles in skin. Ingold devotes the least amount of words to this sub-category, but his focus on the relation between the crease-lines in a palm and the wayfaring approach to reading the "visual map of life" is worth noting. For Ingold, the crease-lines in palm are expressive of "habitual gestures of the hand" (47).

The final class is ghostly lines, which include mathematical, metaphysical, and visionary lines. The astronomical lines among constellations of stars, the mathematically-projected lines of geometrical equations, and the meridian lines of acupuncture—all are examples of ghostly lines. An example of ghostly lines explicitly associated with both writing and rhetoric is the vertical-visual lines about which Richard Lanham writes in his book, *Analyzing Prose*, about which I will write again shortly.

When we begin from the premise that writing is inextricably linked to an expressive force that generates simultaneously a unique and dynamically-related line and a surface, and that each type of writing is transductive because of the specific kinds of physical energy that it converts, the lines constitutive of a physical computing project seem much more writerly than before. Based on Ingold's theory of lines, for a distant writer, the goal is to generate surface-lines that are expressive of transduced, allegorized energy.

To help explain what I mean are two additional sources. The first is Richard Lanham's discussion of the "vertical-visual coordinate" in style, which Ingold might associate with his ghostly line. The second is Sarah Arroyo's notion of the choric swipe, which is inspired by Gregory Ulmer's theory of *choral writing*.

Easily passed over at the bottom of a page in the middle of Richard Lanham's book, *Analyzing Prose*, is an intriguing, albeit tentatively offered, stylistic theory of prose writing. It is in a chapter aptly titled "Styles Seen," but the theory is presented as more of an aside, something slipped in and unrelated to the main themes in that chapter; moreover, it is bookended by qualifiers. Lanham asks,

> The rhetorical tradition has always recognized patterns—chiasmus, for example—which have been called figures of shape, just as figures of sound like alliteration have always been acknowledged. Might we argue that, in wider and more frequent ways, prose styles call upon our powers of visual understanding without seeming to? (97)

It is an intriguing question because Lanham is preoccupied with the role of "the visual" in prose writing throughout his book. It is clear from his introduction, his analytical approach, and his choice of examples, that he's been building to this proposition, even while he puts it in a relatively inconspicuous part of the book.

To appreciate the power of the visual in his book, his analytical method is a case in point. His method is based on a series of visually-appealing diagrams of the schematic patterns by which various prose styles both distinguish themselves and through which they appeal to their audiences. For example, his analysis of the following passage from *To the Lighthouse*, in which Virginia Woolf answers the question, "But what after all is one night?," Lanham includes a visualization of the stylistic structure. The following paragraph from Woolf's novel is the first of several on which his analysis is based.

> But what after all is one night? A short space, especially when the darkness dims so soon, and so soon, a bird sings, a cock crows, or a faint green quickens, like a turning leaf, in the hollow of the wave. Night, however succeeds to night. The winter holds a pack of them in store and deals them equally evenly, with indefatigable fingers. They

length; they darken. Some of them hold aloft clear planets, plates of brightness. The autumn trees, ravaged as they are, take on the flash of tattered flags kindling in the gloom of cool cathedral caves where gold letters on marble pages describe death in battle and how bones bleach and burn far away in Indian sands. The autumn trees gleam in the yellow moonlight, in the light of harvest moons, the light which mellows the energy of labour, and smooths the stubble, and brings the wave lapping blue to the shore. (14)

Lanham's first visualization of the passage is the following:

> . . . the darkness *dims* so soon
>   so soon a bird *sings*
>   a cock *crows*
>   or a faint green *quickens*
>   like a leaf turning
>   in the hollow
>   of the wave.
> Night, however, *succeeds* to night.
>   The winter *holds* a pack of them
>   in store and
>   *deals* them equally, evenly,
>   with indefatigable fingers.
>   They *lengthen*;
>   they *darken*.

The spacing and colorizing of the phrases and words are meant to accentuate the "vertical-visual" coordinate, the ghostly line that is expressive of the rhythm, sound, and sequence of the words.

Farther into his analysis, Lanham presents a visualization of Woolf's use of *chiasmus*:

> A   B   B   A
> Yellow moon*light*, in the *light* of harvest moons
>
> A   B   B   A
> Darkness dims *so soon*, and *so soon* a bird sings

With each visualization, Lanham is foregrounding the vertical-visual coordinate that stylistic choices generate implicitly.

Toward the end of the chapter, "Styles Seen," Lanham speculates that his visualizations may represent more than a useful analytical technique for studying style: "doesn't the technique work just because there is imagistic information already in the prose, information which is suppressed by customary prose presentation?" (97). Lanham is not willing to offer a definitive answer to his question, but we might offer the following response.

Based on Ingold's theory of writing, we can begin by asking about the surface to which the ghostly, visual-vertical lines are associated. If we think of the stylistic points of reference to which Lanham's visualizations relate, a novel, an audio-temporal surface is generated of which the ghostly lines are expressive (and associated). From within the disembodied medium of print-based prose, stylistic schemes in particular generate a novel surface through the association of similar sounds and rhythms. Like the lines that are drawn to and from each star in a constellation, the visual-vertical line that Lanham intuits in the passage by Woolf implies an audio-temporal surface or body (in the Spinozist-Deleuzian) sense. The kinds of prose styles that Lanham charts can be read as a nascent form of distant writing because style is used indirectly as a form of manual inscription. Like a visual algorithm that generates lines on a computer screen, schemes are an indirect way of bringing the hand of writing back to the otherwise disembodied medium of print-based, alphabetic prose.

From Ghostly Lines to Choric Swipes

Moving on from Lanham's ghostly lines is Arroyo's exploration of the choric swipe. Her video, "Choric Swipe," begins with the gestural swipe popularized by multi-touch NUIs such as the *iPad*. She explains that the *iPad* limits the possibilities of choric swiping because "it is still static and the body focuses in on the device, instead of looking through to the multiple possibilities that could emerge" (Arroyo). She continues, explaining that if we move beyond the surface of the tablet, the swipe loses all associations with the more restrictive notion of a *topos*, or a fixed place, empowering us to explore a fuller range of inventional possibilities related to gesturing. In the following quote, she implies that alphabetic writing is symptomatic of the limits against which she is working:

> By disconnecting the swipe from the table (and by association *topos*), [and] moving it toward the *chora*, we see how it holds inventional potential—potential that releases writing from interfaces reliant on letters and symbols and opens up symbiotic relationships with writing, the body, and performative platforms (Arroyo n. pag.)

When the swipe is disconnected from a specific place, its expressiveness can lead to a wide range of surfaces.

Toward the end of her video, Arroyo argues that transparent or see-through touch-screen surfaces serving augmented reality applications (see

A Call for Distant (Transductive) Writing

Figure 49 below) are a way forward for choric swiping on flat surfaces. She says, "Swiping on windows and glass instead of tablets and tables allows for a larger notion of choric grasping to occur. Inventions are evoked rather than found" (Arroyo).

Figure 49. Clip from Arroyo's "Choric Swipe." Video credit: Sarah Arroyo.

Just as with Ingold's theory of writing, the value of Arroyo's choric swipe is that the (manual) gesture is not reduced to a representational role. Compared to Lanham's ghostly lines, the choric swipe draws surface-lines that are unimpeded by the flat screen or the tablet. The transparent surfaces promote a form of way(ve)faring that redefines writing-as-line as a creative and suasive expression—and one that reconnects writing to the *chora*.

For distant writers, the redefinition of writing as a way(ve)faring inscription expressive of a unique dynamic between surface and line is the basis for a move beyond what Harris has characterized as the "tyranny of the alphabet." It's an important opportunity to associate writing with an experimental tradition that values writing as a generative, material, and creative force. In an era of physical computing in which the alphabet is a marginal agent of innovation—and based on a history of writing-as-line—distant writers have a chance to expand the definition of composition. The lines comprising circuits and NUI surfaces are two ways in which distant writing moves beyond our logocentric tradition.

Ghostly Lines in the PC

As a way of concluding this chapter on distant writing, I offer a reading of Victor J. Vitanza's argument in "Abandoned to Writing." Vitanza offers distant writers (and transductive rhetors) the kind of "big picture" mindset that is needed to understand how writing can be practiced at a distance from speech and the alphabet. The following quote is one of my favorites, for reasons that will become clear shortly:

> Writing, however, is not ||||||||||||||||| (barcodes) nor is it //////////////// (slashing of value). Only writers spawned by institutions write in this manner! Rhetoric||||||||||||||||| . . . //////////////Composition.
>
>   Rather, writing is~~~~~~~~~~ ~~~~~ ~~~~~~~~ ~~~~ ~~~~~~~~~~ ~~~~~ ~~~~~~~~~~ ~~~~~ ~~~~~. . . . ("Abandoned")

In the opening paragraphs of his essay, Vitanza claims that there is a direct relation between the repression or marginalization of an idea and its eventual return. His reasons for making this claim are related to the marginalization of experimental, post-disciplinary, "extracurricular" forms of both writing and rhetoric in which he's interested. More than a decade since its publication, in advance of an irrepressible wave of post-PC computing initiatives associated with physical computing, one diacritical mark in particular stands out in a new mode of relief: the tilde. In my reading, the tilde is expressive of physical energy.

Nearly a decade ago, when I first read his essay, I assumed that the more than two-hundred ~s in his essay were a way of allegorizing visually the repressed potential of writing (and rhetoric) in our field, which he called a third "wayve" forward. Now, I read those ~s as a symptom of our field's computational limitations. The provocative choice of the ~s in his essay are an irrepressible sign of the digital era that has been rising all around us. The ~s are a sign of all kinds of forms of physical energy, including electricity, with which computational invention is currently engaged. The new era of computing in which we find ourselves is one in which the digital is not enough; today, it needs the analog.

In 2003, for a special issue of *Enculturation* titled "Rhetoric/Composition: Intersections/Impasses/Differends," Vitanza was invited by the editors to respond to the following question: "What is the place of rhetoric in composition today?" Considering how loaded that question is for scholars associated with a field that, depending on our training and institutional investments, is known affectionately as "Rhet/Comp" or "Comp/Rhet," we shouldn't be surprised by Vitanza's response. Rather than answer the editors' question, which, Vitanza implies, leads typically to the kind of argumentative impasse epitomized by the two positions in the published de-

A Call for Distant (Transductive) Writing

bate between Peter Elbow and David Bartholomae, Vitanza responds with a question of his own: "What is it that writing wants?" (2). For Vitanza, the hostage in the never-ending negotiations of rhet/comp vs. comp/rhet is a more expansive view of what writing can be. In the following excerpt from his essay, Vitanza moves beyond the expressivist/social-epistemic impasse by introducing what he calls a third "wayve" forward:

> Perhapless, there are two possibilities here: "We" can start teaching writing precisely as the university needs it taught. or "we" can attempt "to teach" writing the way "we" want. But there are, let us not forget, third (interval) wayves. And therefore, "we" should ask: What is it that writing wants? I suspect that "writing" does not want what either the uni-versity thinks it needs nor what "we" think we want. ("Abandoned to Writing")

The two sides in the debate between Bartholomae and Elbow are hard to ignore. Bartholomae advocates writing for the university; Elbow advocates for the individual writer. For Vitanza, these two positions are a "hapless" problem because a more expansive approach to what writing can be has been slashed away and ignored. Sometimes, it takes a "bye"-stander or "third party" to ask the obvious question: "why don't you just ask writing what it wants?," which is a position that Vitanza had realized in his scholarly work on another subject, the sophists. In the following excerpt, he offers an admission of how he realized the futility of a reclamatory approach to history and its consequences, and what happens when we do:

> I used to think that the Sophists (sophistic rhetorics) had to be reclaimed "in" the history of rhetoric, or histories of rhetorics, when it became ever so unclearly to me, as Stanley Rosen insists, that the more third sophistic "writing" is suppressed, the stronger and the more a stealthy-rhetoric it becomes. The more than anything or "it" becomes suppressed (or repressed or oppressed) the more "it" eternally returns to have, as some would say, its revenge. (Think of the revenge of the crystal, or the object!) It is, however, non-reactionary re-venge, since nonhuman. ("Abandoned to Writing")

The more we slash away a position, the stronger it returns, albeit not the way we expected. Vitanza realized that a (third) sophistic rhetoric shouldn't be constrained to a prepositional relation with any term; and so, neither should writing. Lost in the endless debates about what writing is, is what writing "wants," what it desires.

For Vitanza, writing is an irrepressible, "non-human" force. The first epigraph preceding his essay offers a sense of his non-human vision of writing. Excerpted from Virginia Woolf's novel, *The Waves*, is a description of the ocean at daybreak: "the [sea] became barred with thick strokes moving, one after another, beneath the surface, following each other, pursuing each other, perpetually" (qtd. in Vitanza). A writer's cursive strokes and the thick strokes moving beneath the surface of the water are both forms of writing; so, while we debate whether a | or a / should be used to separate rhetoric from writing, the ~s are following a course below the surface of our attention.

Rereading Vitanza's essay, the third wayve about which Vitanza wrote now seems like a secret manifesto about the third, digital era of computing in which we now find ourselves. His argument against the use of /s and |s can be reread as a call to move past the exclusive focus on the digital (the |s and /s of binary thinking). And while he used the tildes to allegorize the irrepressible desire of a writing that writes itself through us, I think about the ways in which a new irrepressible era of hybrid, everted computing was writing itself through him, secretly baking itself into his argument. Who better than a scholar of the third wayve, trapped by little more than historic circumstance within a PC era, to channel, unbeknownst to him, the new, wav(y)e-like age of analog? The tildes are now an implicit call to write with the analog flows of energy—a creative potential slashed away by digital or binary thinking.

As I reread Vitanza's essay, I was also reminded of sculptor Andy Goldsworthy's works in the documentary, *Rivers and Tides: Working with Time*. I imagine that Vitanza would call Goldsworthy a "wayve" writer. At one point in the documentary, Goldsworthy describes his process as follows: "Growth and change, and the idea of flow in nature. . . . I want to understand that state and that energy that I have in me that I also feel in plants and in the land. The energy in life that is running through, flowing through, the landscape" (Goldsworthy).

All of the "nature sculptures" that Goldsworthy develops in the documentary are meant to melt, decay, or break apart. Each artifact is designed to express the potential of nature that Goldsworthy feels coursing/ writing through him and other aspects of nature. In that way, his works are a provocative form of transduction: they are designed to bracket nature's energy flows in such a way that we witness its transitions from one form to another.

A Call for Distant (Transductive) Writing

Figure 50. One of Andy Goldsworthy's Writing Projects.

One of my favorite works is a large object built from driftwood (see Figure 50). In the documentary, he rushes to complete it before the tide rises, so that it can float away with the currents. He has built it along the edge of a salmon hole where the river and ocean meet. As the tide rises, and the wood structure floats away, the currents turn it around and around, eventually tearing it apart. The wood structure has been rewritten by the desiring currents. The artifact offers us an indirect view of nature's non-human potential, the way in which it wants to write. Goldsworthy the writer has created something that is not meant to be read directly; rather, it is meant to be a conduit for nature's desires. As he watches his structure float off to sea, Goldsworthy states,

> It feels like it is being taken off into another place, taken off into another world or another work. . . . That moment is really part of that cycle of turning. You feel as if you've touched the heart of the place. That's the way of understanding—seeing something you never saw before that was always there but were blind to. (Goldsworthy)

Casuistically stretching Studdert-Kennedy's description of the flow of speech, we could say that Goldsworthy has created a complex vector of forces comprising the articulation of criss-crossing pieces of driftwood, which acts like a conduit for nature's flow—a kind of sensor. As a sensor, his floating sculpture transduces the physical energy of the water and its currents, and as it breaks floats away, turning, and then breaking apart—a novel figure of style—it allegorizes one of the ways in which nature writes through growth and change: the flow of life. Moreover, his distant form of writing can be valued as a casuistically-stretch example of epideictic rhetoric. Extending Rosenfield's discussion of epideictic from Chapter 1, we might say that Goldsworthy's sculpture celebrates the unconcealment of an aspect of reality that has been hidden from view. Goldsworthy is a writer of nature's radiance. He understands how to write with nature in order to bring some of it back in from the "great outdoors."

5.5 Choric Capacitances

Bare Conductive is a relatively new start-up company that was known initially for selling non-toxic, electrically conductive paint, but in 2014, a year after reaching their Kickstarter funding goal, they released the Touch Board, an Arduino-based microcontroller that features a 12-electrode capacitive touch sensor and an onboard MP3 player (see Figure 51). The visualization dashboard in this chapter is based on their technologies.

Figure 51. Touch Board connected to stencil using conductive paint. Photo credit: Bare Conductive.

Toward the end of Chapter 5, I summarized the argument in Sarah Arroyo's video titled "Choric Swipe." In that video, Arroyo argues that NUI gestures on tablet PCs and smart phones, namely the swipe, have the potential to engage users with the inventional possibilities of chora, but they are constrained by the relatively conventional way in which those gestures are defined. In other words, gestures like the swipe are not designed to express an individual user's broader idiosyncratic range of gestural expression. For the time being, NUI-based technologies are caught in the inertia of a PC era, which tends to constrain user input to a representational and instrumental role. Borrowing a term used by N. Katherine Hayles, the novelty of NUI-based gestural technologies is trapped in a skeuomorphic relation with the PC era.

In *How We Became Posthuman*, Hayles introduces her readers to the concept of the skeuomorph, which is "a design feature that is no longer functional in itself but that refers back to a feature that was functional at an earlier time" (17). It is a concept that she borrows from archaeological anthropology. Hayles explains that skeuomorphs are anachronisms that serve social and psychological needs. An example of a skeuomorph is the sound of a shutter click in a digital camera. The skeuomorphic function of the sound testifies to "the social and psychological necessity for innovation to be tempered by replication" (17). Arguably, the choric potential in touch-based NUI technologies is tempered by this need to replicate.

Returning to Arroyo, if we reframe the rhetorical goals of her argument, so they reflect the shift toward post-PC technologies on which this book is focused, she is calling for a move beyond the PC-era constraints of the swipe in current NUI technologies. She is calling for a form of distant writing. Arroyo offers a way beyond the skeuomorphic impasse by turning to transparent glass surfaces. The swiping surfaces on tablets, smartphones, and other PC-based NUI interfaces are opaque; you cannot see through them. The problem with this opacity, Arroyo explains, is that the user focuses myopically on the technology. A transparent surface would enable a user to look past the opaque surface to more broadly engage with the creative capacities of their gestures. Arroyo explains,

> We can more easily see choric invention happening on glass and windows, so the body, technology, and geography are all brought together. . . . Swiping on windows and glass instead of tablets and tables allows for a larger notion of choric grasping to occur. (Arroyo).

While I would agree that a transparent surface has the potential to broaden the choric relation with swiping, opacity is not the problem. The problem is that the surfaces on which NUI gestures are performed are uniformally smooth and flat. While a "larger notion" of choric grasping can occur in the engagement with a uniformally smooth, flat surface, a deeper, choric engagement can more easily be promoted by experimenting with the sensor-based technology on which touch-screens are typically based, which is the capacitive touch sensor. This is because a capacitive touch sensor can be extended to almost any surface, including your skin; so, there's no reason to constrain it to the smooth, flat screen.

Capacitance is a term that describes the amount of energy a capacitor can store. In an electronic circuit, the component that collects, stores, and discharges a specified amount of electricity is a capacitor. Dustyn Roberts offers the following lay definition of a capacitor, likening it to a water tower:

Choric Capacitances

> A capacitor is like [a] water tower. . . When there's plenty of water around, it gets pumped up to the water tower and stored for later use. When there's a shortage, and the pump stops bring in water, the water tower can drain immediately and supply the water it was storing. Capacitors store electrical energy like water towers store water. (112)

A capacitor's ability to store and discharge electricity is due to its design. Inside the component are two conductive plates separated by a non-conductive material, the dielectric. When positive electrons "stick" to one of the conductive plates, they attract negative electrons to the other plate. The differential is the basis for both storage and discharge.

Based on this design, a capacitive touch sensor uses the natural capacitance of the human body as one of two conductive materials; the other is one of the sensor's inputs. When you touch an electrode, or the conductive paint extending from it, you lower the voltage in the circuit. When that occurs, it is transduced into a digital value.

The Touch Board offers digital rhetors and distant writers twelve inputs with which to work. Additionally, the conductive paint can be written in ways that have the effect of multiplying the number of inputs. Whereas all of the surfaces that Arroyo cites are flat and smooth, conductive paint can be applied to a wide range of surfaces. It can be drawn across floors, walls, ceilings, furniture, and the human body. The flexibility of the paint-as-medium makes it possible to create a "post human" electric circuit comprising one or more humans whose engagements with each other, the walls, floor, and objects in the room evert the conventional experience of touch. Those eversions can lead to deeper, choric engagements.

In Figure 52, a dancer with conductive paint on her hands, legs, and feet engages a series of circuit designs embedded in the walls and floor of "The Music Box." Her engagements are the basis for a musical performance. In a description of the performance published online, the designers explain, "as different parts of her body touched its surface, musical notes and patterns were created. The result of this direct interaction between movement and sound was a unique and compelling performance" (Seth).

Suasive Iterations

Figure 52. Screen capture of dancer performing in "The Music Box." Photo credit: SIDeR09: Flirting with the Future.

The performance was part of the 5th Student Interaction Design Research Conference in 2009, SIDeR09: Flirting with the Future. For a digital writer engaged in choric invention, transduction occurs both in the software and in the painted circuit designs extending from the electrodes in a capacitive

Choric Capacitances

touch sensor. In fact, the design of the conductive paint could allegorize a visual form of style. Depending on the surfaces on which the painted shapes and lines are drawn, the rhetor-writer (and the performer) could engage in a form of way(ve)faring about which Ingold and Vitanza write, which would further resonate with the conductive aspects of choric writing.

Designing a Basic Interface

In Figure 53, I developed a basic interface using Bare Conductive's Touch Board, alligator test leads, and copper foil tape. The Touch Board is fastened to the back of the cardboard, the capacitive touch leads sticking out on the bottom left. The multi-colored test leads are clipped from each of the pins on the Touch Board to strips of 5mm copper tape. Copper tape is an inexpensive conductive material to use during the initial steps toward a transductive strategy. It can stripped and reapplied, and you do not have to wait for it to dry.

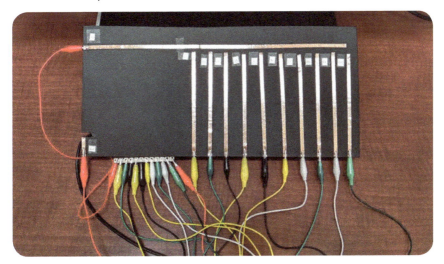

Figure 53. Copper-tape interface for exploring capacitive touch interface.

     Once a software program is written that transduces the sensory data from the twelve inputs in ways that can lead to an everted experience, the tape can be replaced with conductive paint, which can be extended in some of the ways suggested above. For example, a project could be developed that adds an interactive dimension to artist Damon Davis's work #AllHandsOnDeck. Davis's work comprises a series of hands photographed palms-down against a white background. Large-scale prints of them are wallpapered around Ferguson, Missouri. In Figure 54, Davis stands in front of a store front where a few of his prints are wallpapered.

Figure 54. Artist Damon Davis (center) standing in front of #AllHandsOn-Deck. Photo credit: GlobalGrindTV.

The work was developed initially in response to the shooting death of Michael Brown. As an artist, Davis collaborated on a response to the incident and its aftermath. As he explains in the following quote, the work was meant to support the local community of volunteers and activists in Ferguson who promoted the ongoing work associated with #blacklivesmatter:

> The hands you see are images I have captured of people who have shaped and upheld this movement. The peoples movement. It is our right—to be seen, to be heard . . . to be validated. It is our collective responsibility. The "All Hands On Deck" project is an ode to that diverse collective dedicated to protecting our human rights, no matter race, age or gender. "All Hands On Deck" is our charge—a call of action to stand with those who stand for us all. (Davis).

One way in which to turn Davis's prints into a physical computing project is the following: conductive paint underneath the hand prints wallpapered to a wall could be used to transduce any user interactions with the hand prints toward a rhetorical end. When a passersby puts one or both hands on top of one of the prints—and depending on how hard they press their hands, to the wall—the input to the Touch Board associated with that event could play one or more audio tracks. The choice of tracks could be based on a wide range of factors: whether the participant placed one or both hands on the print, the time of day (or night) when she interacted with the wall, or whether she was alone (were there more than two input engaged simultaneously). Participatory engagements could be transduced in a wide

Choric Capacitances

range of ways that contribute to a choric engagement with #blacklivesmatter and related civil rights issues associated with your city. Toward this end, the tracks could be excerpts from recent podcasts about #blacklivesmatters, recordings of young African American men talking candidly about their hopes and fears growing up in America, or, more ominously, a police officer ordering you to put your hands on the wall and spread your legs. The audio tracks could be saved to the Touch Board, or they could be pulled directly from a database of sound files in the cloud. If they are pulled from the cloud, they could be updated to stay current with national news stories.

A Visualization Dashboard for the Touch Board

Figure 55 is a screen shot of the visualization dashboard for the Touch Board's inputs. As with the previous three dashboards, it is just one possible way in which to explore the transductive potentials of the technology. In the bottom-right corner of the dashboard is a real-time visualization of the analog data values associated with each of the electrodes. From bottom to top, the row of alphanumerics, E0-E11, represent the twelve electrodes on the Touch Board. In Figure 53 above, each line of copper tape has an E# next to it. The numbers and bar graph above each electrode are their analog values. The analog data range, which is an integer value, extends from -3 to 500. Depending on the conductivity of the material extending from the electrode, the upper range will vary. Of note: you do not have to touch the copper tape to register a value. A body's capacitance can affect a value from an inch or more away.

Figure 55. Visualization dashboard for Bare Conductive's Touch Board.

Suasive Iterations

The dashboard itself is divided among four columns. In the column on the left, a transductive experiment was prototyped using four electrodes, E1, E7, E2, and E8. If E1 and E7 or E2 and E8 are activated beyond a pre-defined threshold, an event is triggered. The event could invoke a sound, image, text, or other media object. If all four electrodes are activated beyond a specified threshold, a third type of event is triggered (Event C). Related to the idea of creating an interactive version of Damon's activist art project described above, depending on how and where the conductive paint is drawn in the event space, the transduction that occurs could contribute to an everted experience in which an object, person, image, or text fragment is associated with an experience that transforms how the moment is conventionally understood.

In the second column from the left, an event is triggered (or terminated) when one of the four electrodes are activated, E1, E2, E7, E8. In the third column, one of four events is triggered, depending on the value associated with E4. In the fourth column, which is further divided among six rows, values from five different electrodes are mapped to a series of different ranges. The point of the mapped values is to demonstrate the extent to which the value from an electrode, which represents a range of approximately -3 to 500, can be transduced to the range of the alphabet (0-25), a range of grayscale values (50-255), 1080 degrees of rotation along the Z axis, a range that rescales the size of an ellipse (5-65), or to a Boolean value. In the row at the bottom, an average value for all of the electrodes is displayed on the left. On the right is the sum total of all of the values.

Any of these transductions can be the basis for stylistic allegorizations that lead to a novel eversion of the space. For the digital writer exploring the choric potential of capacitive touch sensory data and conductive paint, the combination of code-based transductions and line-making practices are an opportunity to move well-beyond the skeuomorphic inertia of PC-based NUI swipes and other forms of touch.

6 After the Bookish Era of the PC

As I was drafting this final chapter, I took a break to stream director Spike Jonze's film *Her* a couple of years after its release. I had known that I would have to watch it before I finished drafting this book because it takes place in a not-so-distant future in which NUI-based technologies predominate. The main storyline of *Her* is about the relationship between Theodore and Samantha. Theodore is a private, somewhat lonely man. Samantha is a new kind of operating system (OS)—an artificial intelligence who manages all aspects of his life. A few scenes into the film, they have fallen in love with each other.

The backdrop for their relationship is a post-PC techno-culture. Theodore, his friends, and passerby in the subway or on the street are constantly engaged with one or more voice- and gesture-based NUI technologies. As the film follows Theodore from work to home, we watch how he accesses his music, email, and social media accounts through voice-actuated commands and requests. When he arrives home, most of the interfaces for his appliances and systems are voice- or gesture-based. Some are based on some kind of ambient sensor technology. For example, the lights in each of the rooms in his apartment turn on automatically as he walks in to them. Theodore's world is one in which NUI-based everywares are ubiquitous. It's an epitomization of Greenfield's everywares.

But a few scenes into the film, it is apparent that most of *Her* is, nonetheless, about personal computing. NUI-based technologies are an important aspect of *Her*, but the techno-culture depicted in *Her* is thoroughly PC-based. Evidence of a PC-era storyline include the following. First, the film implicitly depicts a techno-culture in which distinctions are upheld between the virtual realm of the computer and the "real" world. For example, Samantha, the operating system's artificial intelligence, yearns to have a body and to join Theodore in the real world. Also, the "real" world seems somewhat empty and lifeless. Theodore and most of the extras in scenes depicting public life are self-absorbed in their interactions with their PCs. The techno-culture in *Her* may be NUI-based, but the relationships with technology are centripetal or introverting, which is a symptom of the extent to which user's must forego the "real" world in order to participate in the virtual. A final evidential point is that Theodore's new operating system epitomizes Weiser's description of a "dramatic machine." Samantha is designed to hold all of Theodore's attention. In fact, the OS is so adept at winning his attention that Theodore falls in love with it.

Suasive Iterations

And yet, there is a provocative twist on the question of personal computing toward the end of the film. In one of the final scenes, Theodore is forced to grapple with an issue related to post-correlationism. Theodore and the artificial intelligence Samantha are in love with each other, but it occurs to Theodore that Samantha may be involved with other people. In the following excerpt, Theodore queries Samantha about her devotion to him.

> THEODORE. Do you talk to anyone else while we're talking?
> SAMANTHA. Yes.
> THEODORE. Are you talking to anyone else right now—any other people or OSs or anything?
> SAMANTHA. Yeah.
> THEODORE. How many others?
> SAMANTHA. 8,316. (Jonze, *Her*)

As Theodore mentally processes the number, he watches passersby interacting with their artificial intelligences. Theodore continues his questioning: "Are you in love with anyone else?" Samantha replies somewhat obliquely, "I've been trying to figure out how to talk to you about this." Theodore follows up, "How many?" Samantha confesses, "641." The dialogue ends soon after Samantha's confession. Theodore is confused, hurt, and struggling to make sense of his feelings. It seems that Theodore has realized that some of those passersby may be talking to the same AI, albeit different versions of it. In fact, there may only be one AI. The scene ends with the following four lines of dialogue, which dramatize an issue that I introduced in Chapter 3.

> THEODORE. I thought you were mine.
> SAMANTHA. I still am yours. . . . I'm different from you.
> THEODORE. You're mine or you're not mine.
> SAMANTHA. No, Theodore. I'm yours and I'm not yours.

For Theodore, love is self-centered, personal, and its value is binary: "You're mine or you're not mine." But for a cloud-based AI with unlimited reach and processing power, there is a "great outdoors" beyond any one user with whom she is engaged. Harkening back to something Bogost had written about, which I quoted in Chapter 3, Theodore is grappling with the realization that he does not sit "at the center of being, organizing and regulating it like an ontological watchmaker" (Bogost 5). In fact, extending some of Bogost's words in *Alien Phenomenology*, as Theodore is confronted by Samantha's ontology, the ebb of the "epistemological tide" (Bogost 5) reveals the iridescent shells of the post-PC era. *Her* may be, for the most part,

After the Bookish Era of the PC

a film about personal computing, but the climax is a poignant dramatization of the limits of that perspective, due to the ways in which it blinds us to the post-human reality toward which the era of everywares and physical computing are fast heading.

As I was watching *Her*, I was reminded of something about which I argued in an earlier chapter. In Chapter 1, I called the PC era fairly bookish. Looking at it from the new post-PC era, the PC era seems to have supported and served our print-centric, disciplinary goals. The boundaried, two-dimensional screen resembles the printed page, the keyboard reinforces the importance of phonetic thought and alphabetic writing, and our handheld tablets and smart phones are in the general shape and size of trade books. So what happens when technologies like the screen and keyboard are replaced by wires, solder, various kinds of microcomponents, Ohm's Law, and the principle of transduction? If many of the materials, technologies and processes associated with the new computational era are not easily reconciled with the GUI- and PC-based technologies conventionally associated with digital work in our field, and if they do not reconcile that easily with the print-centric traditions on which our discipline is persistently based, can we call ourselves and our projects rhetorical or writerly? The answer I've offered in this book is yes. It may take a bit of casuistic stretching, but we absolutely can call ourselves digital rhetors and writers when we leave the PC-era polis for the uncountry of the physical.

Related to this final point is a concern that has come up in a few of my graduate seminars of late. When I teach or mentor graduate students on physical computing projects, I usually have to address a certain level of concern that manifests itself as a question: will this kind of work count as scholarship on my CV? The worry is a valid one. Should graduate students in rhetoric and writing who are vying for a tenure-track position, or junior faculty working toward tenure, expect projects like these to count as scholarly publications in the eyes of their departments and professional fields? My response is yes, albeit with the following qualification. These projects are best developed with two audiences in mind. One audience is the public, because many of these kinds of works can be developed for public venues, or installed in public settings. As such, they are "extra-curricular" contributions to novel, interdisciplinary work. They can help establish you as a digital scholar, as a public intellectual and maker, but some colleagues may find it difficult to reconcile them with a traditional sense of scholarship. But the second audience is scholarly because the data these works can capture, and the ways in which audience engagements with these works can be studied, can be the basis for publications about the new, post-PC era of popular computing. For example, the project outlined in Chapter 5.5 could

Suasive Iterations

be fully developed to support an article that contributes ultimately to the scholarship on chora. Let us say that I want to write an article in response to Thomas Rickert's and Sarah Arroyo's contributions to the scholarship on chora. To that end, I decide to develop a physical computing project, which will serve as part of my supporting argument. I install my interactive work in a public space, and then I record and document the data and user engagements with it. The data leads me to some insights about the ways in which chora can be theorized, due to the ways in which users have engaged with it. The public showing (and any press associated with it) is added to my CV, and the data and documentation from the installation is used in the article that I submit to a journal in my field. You might consider the use of the data and documentation as a kind of scientific approach to scholarly publication: you ran an experiment, analyzed the data, and you are now publishing your findings in support of an argument that contributes to the scholarly conversation in your field.

Perhaps there will be a time in the not-so-distant future when physical computing projects will be recognized as "stand-alone" scholarship. Certainly, some "born digital" work in the humanities is recognized as such. Until that day fully arrives, I hope that more digital rhetors and distant writers will take a chance and break through the looking glass of the PC era in order to experience the way in which audiences can be moved or suaded in new and compelling ways by creating everted realities from stylistic allegorizations of our transduced world.

Works Cited

Aristotle. *The Art of Rhetoric*. Trans. John H. Freese. Cambridge (Mass.): Harvard UP, 1975. Print.

Arroyo, Sarah J. "The Choric Swipe." *YouTube*, 18 May 2012. Web. 1 Aug. 2016.

Banzi, Massimo. *Getting Started with Arduino*. Sebastopol: O'Reilly Media, 2009. Print.

Basu, Moni. "Artist Brings Beauty to a Scarred Ferguson." *CNN.com*. Cable News Network, 21 Nov. 2014. Web. 1 Aug. 2016.

Baudrillard, Jean, Philip Beitchman, W G. J. Niesluchowski, and Jim Fleming. *Fatal Strategies: Crystal Revenge*. Semiotext(e), 1990. Print.

Belcove, Julie L. "Steamy Wait Before a Wall in a Museum's Rain." *The New York Times* 18 July 2013: A1. Print.

Bernstein, Mark. "Patterns of Hypertext." *Eastgate*. Eastgate Systems, Inc., n.d. Web. 1 Aug. 2016.

Berg. "#Flock, with TwitterUK." *Berg*. N.p., n.d. Web. 17 Sept. 2015.

Bevan, David and Brendan Dawes. "Crushed Under Sodium Lights." *Born Magazine* 2002. Web. 1 Aug. 2016.

Bitzer, Lloyd F. "The Rhetorical Situation." *Philosophy and Rhetoric* 1.1 (1968): 1-14. Print.

Blanciak, François. *Siteless: 1001 Building Forms*. Cambridge, Mass: MIT P, 2008. Print.

Blum, Jeremy. "Tech Bits 13–Analog and Digital Signals." *YouTube*, 20 June 2010. Web. 1 Aug. 2016.

Bodmer, Paul. "Is It Pedagogy or Administrative? Administering Distance Delivery to High Schools." *Delivering College Composition: The Fifth Canon*. Ed. Kathleen Blake Yancey. Portsmouth, NH: Boynton/Cook Publishers, 2006. 115–126. Print.

Bogost, Ian. *Alien Phenomenology, Or, What It's Like to Be a Thing*. Minneapolis: U of Minnesota P, 2012. Print.

—. *Persuasive Games: The Expressive Power of Videogames*. Cambridge, Mass: MIT P, 2007. Print.

—. *Unit Operations: An Approach to Video Game Criticism*. Cambridge, MA: MIT P, 2006. Print.

Brock, Kevin. "Enthymeme as Rhetorical Algorithm." *Present Tense: A Journal of Rhetoric in Society* 4.1 (2014): n. pag. Web.

Brooke, Collin Gifford. *Lingua Fracta: Toward a Rhetoric of New Media*. Cresskill, NJ: Hampton P, 2009. Print.

Works Cited

Bryant, Levi. "Correlationism and the Fate of Philosophy." *Larval Subjects.* N.p., 13 June 2008. Web. 1 Aug. 2016.

Burke, Kenneth. *Attitudes Toward History.* 3rd ed., Berkeley: U of California P, 1984. Print.

Carruthers, Mary. *The Book of Memory: A Study of Memory in Medieval Culture.* Cambridge, UK: Cambridge UP, 2008. Print.

Coleridge, Samuel T, Henry N. Coleridge, Edward F. Finden, and Thomas Phillips. *Specimens of the Table Talk of the Late Samuel Taylor Coleridge. in Two Volumes.* London: John Murray, 1835. Print.

"Computing, Naturally." *Microsoft News Center.* Microsoft Corporation, 2 Mar. 2010. Web. 1 Aug. 2016.

Cope, Edward M. *An Introduction to Aristotle's Rhetoric: With Analysis, Notes and Appendices.* London: Macmillan, 1966. Print.

Cramer, Florian. *Words Made Flesh: Code, Culture, Imagination.* Rotterdam, Netherlands: Piet Zwart Institute, 2005. Web.

Dear Esther. The Chinese Room, 2012. Video game.

DeLanda, Manuel. *Intensive Science and Virtual Philosophy.* New York, NY: Continuum Impacts, 2005. Print.

Deleuze, Gilles. *Spinoza, Practical Philosophy.* Trans. Robert Hurley. San Francisco: City Lights Books, 1988. Print.

De los Reyes, August. "Predicting the Past." *Web Directions South.* N.p., 25 Sept. 2008. Web. 1 August 2016.

"Digital Humanities Manifesto 2.0." N.p., 22 Jun. 2009. Web. 1 August 2016.

"Digital Humanities Start-Up Grants." *NEH Office of Digital Humanities.* National Endowment for the Humanities, n.d. Web. 1 August 2016.

Dourish, Paul and Genevieve Bell. *Divining a Digital Future: Mess and Mythology in Ubiquitous Computing.* Cambridge, MA: MIT P, 2014. Print.

Edbauer, Jenny. "Unframing Models of Public Distribution: From Rhetorical Situation to Rhetorical Ecologies." *Rhetoric Society Quarterly* 35.4 (Fall 2005): 5-24. Print.

Ekman, Ulrik, ed. *Throughout: Art and Culture Emerging with Ubiquitous Computing.* Cambridge, MA: MIT P, 2012. Print.

Fahnestock, Jeanne. *Rhetorical Style: The Uses of Language in Persuasion.* Cary, NC: Oxford UP, 2011. Print.

"Fastest-Selling Gaming Peripheral." *Officially Amazing Guinness World Records.* Guinness World Records, Jan. 2011. Web. 1 Aug. 2016.

Frazer, James George. *The Golden Bough: A Study in Magic and Religion.* Hertfordshire, UK: Wordsworth Editions Ltd, 2008. Print.

Galloway, Alexander R. and Eugene Thacker. *The Exploit: A Theory of Networks.* Minneapolis: U of Minnesota P, 2007. Print.

Works Cited

Gates, Bill. "The Power of the Natural User Interface." *The Gates Notes*. N.p., 28 Oct. 2011. Web. 1 Aug. 2016.

Gibson, William. *Burning Chrome*. New York: HarperCollins Publishers, 2003. Print.

—. "Google's Earth." *The New York Times* 1 Sept. 2010: A23. Print.

Gil, Jose. "Paradoxical Body." *Planes of Composition: Dance, Theory, and the Global*. Eds. Andre Lepecki and Jenn Joy. London: Seagull Books, 2010. 85–106. Print.

Good Night Lamp. "Good Night Lamp." *Vimeo*. January 2013. Web. 1 August 2013.

Greenfield, Adam. *Everyware: The Dawning Age of Ubiquitous Computing*. San Francisco, CA: New Riders Publishing, 2006. Print.

Greenspan, Alan. "Technological Advances and Productivity." Remarks at the 80th Anniversary Rewards Dinner of the Conference Board. 16 October 1996. Web. 1 August 2016.

Harman, Graham. "Ontography: The Rise of the Objects." *Object-Oriented Philosophy*. N.p., 14 July 2009. Web. 1 Aug. 2016.

Harris, Roy. *The Origin of Writing*. La Salle, IL: Open Court, 1986. Print.

Harvey, David. *The Condition of Postmodernity: An Enquiry into the Origins of Cultural Change*. Oxford, UK: Blackwell Publishers, 2000. Print.

Hayles, Katherine. *How We Became Posthuman: Virtual Bodies in Cybernetics, Literature, and Informatics*. Chicago, IL: U of Chicago P, 1999. Print.

Hill, Adams Sherman. *Principles of Rhetoric*. New York: Harper & Bros., 1882. Print.

Huizinga, Johan. *Homo Ludens: A Study of the Play Element in Culture*. New York: Beacon P, 1971. Print.

Hume, David, David F. Norton, and Mary J. Norton. *A Treatise of Human Nature*. Oxford: Oxford UP, 2000. Print.

Ingold, Tim. *Lines: A Brief History*. London: Routledge, 2007. Print.

Jackson, Shelley. *Patchwork Girl*. Watertown, MA: Eastgate Systems, Inc. 1995. Storyspace file.

Jakobson, Roman. "Two Aspects of Language and Two Types of Aphasic Disburbances." *Language in Literature*. Eds. Krystina Pomorska and Stephen Rudy. Cambridge, MA: The Belknap P of Harvard UP, 1987. Print.

Jones, Steven E. *The Emergence of the Digital Humanities*. New York: Routledge, 2014. Print.

Kendon, Adam. *Gesture: Visible Action as Utterance*. New York: Cambridge UP, 2004. Print.

Kotz, Liz. *Words to Be Looked At: Language in 1960s Art*. Cambridge, MA: MIT P, 2010. Print.

Works Cited

Kress, Gunther. *Before Writing: Rethinking the Paths to Literacy*. New York: Routledge, 1997. Print.

Lanham, Richard A. *The Economics of Attention: Style and Substance in the Age of Information*. Chicago, IL: U of Chicago P, 2006. Print.

—. *Analyzing Prose*. 2nd ed. New York, NY: Bloomsbury Publishing, 2003. Print.

Leroi-Gourhan, André. *Gesture and Speech*. Trans. Anna Bostock Berger. Cambridge, MA: MIT P, 1993. Print.

Levi-Strauss, Claude. *The Savage Mind*. Chicago, IL: University of Chicago P, 1968. Print.

Manovich, Lev. *The Language of New Media*. Cambridge, MA: MIT P, 2001. Print.

McCarthy, Cormac. *The Road*. New York, NY: Vintage Books, 2006. Print.

McCorkle, Ben. *Rhetorical Delivery as Technological Discourse: A Cross-Historical Study*. Carbondale: Southern Illinois UP, 2012. Print.

Meillassoux, Quentin. *After Finitude: An Essay on the Necessity of Contingency*. Trans. Ray Brassier. New York: Continuum, 2008.

Microsoft Game Studios. *Kinect Adventures!* Microsoft Corporation, 2010. XBOX 360.

Montfort, Nick. "Continuous Paper: The Early Materiality and Workings of Electronic Literature." *Nickm.com*. N.p., Jan. 2005. Web. 1 January 2016.

Moretti, Franco. *Graphs, Maps, Trees: Abstract Models for a Literary History*. New York, NY: Verso, 2005.

Munster, Anna. *Materializing New Media: Embodiment in Information Aesthetics*. Hanover, NH: Dartmouth College P, 2006. Print.

Nietzsche, Friedrich. *The Portable Nietzsche*. Trans. Walter Kaufmann. New York: Penguin Books, 1977. Print.

O'Sullivan, Dan and Tom Igoe. *Physical Computing: Sensing and Controlling the Physical World with Computers*. New York, NY: Cengage Learning, 2004. Print.

Perelman, Chaim and Olbrechts-Tyteca Lucie. *The New Rhetoric: A Treatise on Argumentation*. Trans. John Wilkinson and Purcell Weaver. Notre Dame, IN: Notre Dame UP, 1968. Print.

Philostratus and Eunapius. *Philostratus: Lives of the Sophists. Eunapius: Lives of the Philosophers*. Cambridge, MA: Loeb Classical Library, 1921. Print.

Pink, Daniel. *A Whole New Mind: Why Right-Brainers Will Rule the Future*. New York, NY: Riverhead Books, 2006. Print.

Presner, Todd. "Digital Humanities Manifesto 2.0 Launched." *Todd Presner*. N.p., 22 June 2009. Web. 1 August 2013.

Pullman, George. *Writing Online: Rhetoric for the Digital Age*. Indianapolis, IN: Hackett Publishing Company, 2016. Print.

Works Cited

"Pulse-width Modulation." *Wikipedia: The Free Encyclopedia*. Wikimedia Foundation, Inc. 25 July 2013. Web. 1 August 2016.

Rabinovitch, Simona. "2013's Most Instagrammed Art Installations." *Gotham Magazine* Dec. 2013. Web. 1 Aug. 2016.

Ramsay, Stephen. *Reading Machines: Toward an Algorithmic Criticism*. Urbana, IL: U of Illinois P, 2011. Print.

—. "Who's in and Who's Out." *Stephen Ramsay Blog*. 8 January 2011. Web. 1 August 2016.

—. "On Building." *Stephen Ramsay Blog*. 11 January 2011. Web. 1 August 2016.

Random International, "Rain Room." *Random*. N.p., 2012. Web. 1 August 2016.

Ratto, Matt. "Critical Making: Conceptual and Material Studies in Technology and Social Life." *The Information Society: An International Journal* 27:4 (2011): 252-260. Print.

Ridolfo, Jim. "Rhetorical Delivery as Strategy: Rebuilding the Fifth Canon from Practitioner Stories." *Rhetoric Review* 31:2 (2012): 117-129. Print.

—. and Danielle Nicole DeVoss. "Composing for Recomposition: Rhetorical Velocity and Delivery." *Kairos: A Journal of Rhetoric, Technology, and Pedagogy* 13.2 (Spring, 2009): n.pag. Web.

Rivers and Tides: Andy Goldsworthy Working with Time. Dir. Thomas Riedelsheimer. Roxie Releasing, 2001. DVD.

Roberts, Dustyn. *Making Things Move DIY Mechanisms for Inventors, Hobbyists, and Artists*. New York, NY: McGraw-Hill Education, 2010. Print.

Rosenfield, Lawrence W. "The Practical Celebration of Epideictic." *Rhetoric in Transition: Studies in the Nature and Uses of Rhetoric*. Ed. E.E. White. University Park, PA: Pennsylvania State UP, 1980. Print.

Saint Augustine. *Confessions*. Trans. Henry Chadwick. New York: Oxford UP, 2009. Print.

Saper, Craig (dj readies). "Intimate Bureaucracies: A Manifesto." Brooklyn, NY: Punctum Books, 2012. Print.

Selfe, Cynthia and Richard Selfe. "The Politics of the Interface: Power and Its Exercise in Electronic Contact Zones." *College Composition and Communication* 45.4 (2009): 480-504. Print.

Seth, Rhadika. "My Body Paint Communicates with Lights and Music." *YD: Yanko Design*. N.p., 7 Feb 2009. Web. 1 Jan 2016..

Silva Rhetoricae. "Figures of Interruption." *Silva Rhetoricae: The Forest of Rhetoric*. Brigham Young University. 26 Feb. 2007. Web. 13 Dec 2015.

—. "Scheme." *Silva Rhetoricae: The Forest of Rhetoric*. Brigham Young University. 26 Feb. 2007. Web. 13 Dec 2015.

—. "Trope." *Silva Rhetoricae: The Forest of Rhetoric*. Brigham Young University. 26 Feb. 2007. Web. 13 Dec 2015.

Works Cited

Sterne, Lawrence. *The Life and Opinions of Tristram Shandy, Gentleman*. New York: Dover Publications, 2007. Print.

Studdert-Kennedy, Michael. "The Phoneme as a Perceptuomotor Structure." *Language Perception and Production: Relationships Between Listening, Speaking, Reading, and Writing*. Ed. Alan Allport. London: Academic P, 1987. Print.

Team Adafruit. "The Open Kinect project–THE OK PRIZE–get $3,000 bounty for Kinect for Xbox 360 open source drivers." *Adafruit Blog*. Adafruit Industries, Nov. 4, 2010. Web.. 1 Jan. 2016.

Tesla, Nikola. "On Light and Other High Frequency Phenomena." Franklin Institute. Philadelphia, PA. 24 February 1893. Keynote Address. Web. 1 August 2013.

The Matrix. Dir. Andy Wachowski and Lana Wachowski. Warner Brothers, 1999. DVD.

Trimbur, John. "Composition and the Circulation of Writing." *College Composition and Communication* 52.2 (2000): 188-219. Print.

"Twitter UK Presents #Flock." *You Tube*. 17 April 2013. Web. 1 August 2013.

Ulmer, Gregory. *Heuretics: The Logic of Invention*. Baltimore: The Johns Hopkins UP, 1994. Print.

Vitanza, Victor J. *Negation, Subjectivity, and the History of Rhetoric*. Albany: SUNY P, 1997. Print.

—. "Abandoned to Writing: Notes Toward Several Provocations." *Enculturation: A Journal of Rhetoric, Writing, and Culture*. 5.1 (2003): n. pag. Web. 1 August 2013.

Wainwright, Oliver. "Barbican's Rain Room: It's Raining, But You Won't Get Wet." *The Guardian*. 3 October 2012. Web. 1 August 2013.

Walter, E.V. *Placeways: A Theory of the Human Environment*. Chapel Hill: U of North Carolina P, 1988.

Waze – GPS, Maps & Social Traffic. Palo Alto, CA: Waze Inc., 2015. Web.

Weiser, Mark. "The Computer for the 21st Century." *Scientific American*. 265.3 (September 1991): 66-75. Print.

—, and John Seely Brown. "The Coming Age of Calm Technology." Xerox PARC: 1996. Web. 29 December 2015.

Werner, Marta L. "Helen Keller and Anne Sullivan: Writing Otherwise." *Interval(le)s*. II.2 – III.1 (Fall 2008 – Winter 2009): n. pag. Web. 1 August 2013.

Wigdor, Daniel, and Dennis Wixon. *Brave NUI World: Designing Natural User Interfaces for Touch and Gesture*. New York: Morgan Kaufman, 2011. Print.

Woolf, Virginia. *The Waves*. New York: Harcourt Brace Jovanovich, 1978. Print.

Yancey, Kathleen B. "Delivering College Composition: A Vocabulary for Discussion." *Delivering College Composition: The Fifth Canon*. Portsmouth, NH: Boynton/Cook Publishers, 2006. Print.

Index

~, 59, 146, 148
#Flock, 66–67, 87, 93

acceleration, 46, 51–52, 54–55, 110
accelerometer: ADXL 335, 46,
  50–52, 56–57, 59, 60–62, 64
actuators, 6, 10, 12, 14, 21, 27, 31,
  36, 38, 42, 50, 56–57, 63, 67,
  94, 128–129
affective, 16, 110–111, 114, 119
algorithm, 43, 45, 126, 144
Alien Phenomenology (Bogost), 74, 78,
  82, 160
allegorical: microtechnologies,
  6, 23–24, 38, 71; style, 19,
  21, 31–32
allegorized, 19–21, 31–32, 35,
  56, 63, 92–93, 98, 102, 123–
  124, 142
allegorizing, 21, 23, 31, 34–36, 47,
  50, 52, 54–57, 60, 63–64, 90,
  92, 96, 98, 111, 122, 124, 146
alphabet, 22, 131, 133–134,
  145–146, 158; tyranny of, 22,
  129, 134, 145; post-alphabetic,
  72, 128
ambience, 20–21, 34
analog, 4, 6, 10–11, 19, 22, 24–26,
  30–31, 35, 50–52, 54, 57, 60–61,
  66, 120, 129, 134, 146, 148, 157
anti-rhetorical, 24, 67, 69, 75, 94
Arduino, 26–27, 29–30, 38, 50–
  51, 53, 61–63, 92, 94–95
armada, 59–60
Arroyo, Sarah, 72, 142, 144–145,
  151–153, 162
attention, 8, 67–69, 71–73, 75–78,
  83, 86, 90, 112, 148, 159

audience, 14, 16–19, 21, 47, 57–58,
  65, 86–87, 110, 161

Banzi, Massimo, 36, 38, 42, 44
Barbican Gallery, 3–4, 12
Bare Conductive, 27–28, 151, 155,
  157; Touch Board, 27–28, 151,
  153, 155–157
Berg (design firm), 66–67
birds, 66–67, 93, 140
Bitzer, Lloyd, 15–16
Blum, Jeremy, 51
boat: origami, 55, 60–61, 64
body, 12, 14, 24–25, 49, 60–61, 63,
  102–103, 106–111, 114, 118–119,
  122, 126, 140, 144, 152–153,
  157, 159
Bogost, Ian, 24, 67, 74–75, 78–86,
  90, 160
botanize, 31, 35–36, 38, 46, 57
bricolage, 36, 41–42; bricoleur, 38,
  39, 41, 44
Brown, John Seely, 68, 70–71, 156
Bryant, Levi, 74
Bulwer, John, 108
Burke, Kenneth, 14–15, 32, 33;
  casuistic stretching, 15–16, 19,
  31–32, 86, 161
Burroughs,William, 43

calm, 67–72, 75, 86–87, 91, 94;
  encalming, 67–68, 71, 73, 93
camera, 114–115, 151
capacitance, 49, 153, 157
casuistic stretching, 15–16, 19,
  31–32, 86, 161
Charlieplexing, 94–95
chiasmus, 50, 142–143

Index

choric invention, 142, 144–145, 151–154, 157–158

choric, choric engagements, Choric Swipe, 144–145, 151, 162

Cicero, Marcus Tullius, 107–108

circuits, 10, 13, 26, 49, 50, 60, 94, 95, 127–129, 135, 140, 152–154

CLI (Command Line Interface), 111

climax, 21, 82, 161

cloud computing, 8, 12, 14, 44, 50, 90, 99, 157

composition, 8, 14, 21, 67, 69, 72–73, 120, 135, 139, 145–146

computational approach, 4, 14, 127

computational invention, 146

computational thought, 36, 44–45

computing, 3–6, 8, 11–12, 14–16, 19, 21–27, 31, 35, 37–39, 42, 47, 57, 60–62, 67, 69, 70–72, 86, 91–93, 102, 110–111, 128, 135, 142, 145–146, 148, 156, 161–162; personal, 6, 8, 25, 159–161; post-PC, 6, 9, 12, 23, 25, 28, 35, 67–69, 103, 146, 152, 159–161; ubiquitous, 4, 9, 23, 28, 67, 102, 111, 159

conductive paint, 28, 151, 153, 155–156, 158

Copper tape, 155, 157

correlationism, 73–74

Cramer, Florian, 23, 36, 42–45

Davis, Damon, 155–156

DeLanda, Manuel, 118

Deleuze, Gilles, 110, 118–119

delivery: fifth canon, 24, 102–103, 106–109, 111, 114, 119–120

deviation: artful, 21, 34, 57

DeVoss, Danielle Nicole, 103, 109

digital humanities, 15, 21, 127

digital rhetoric, 15, 23–24, 35, 46, 70, 72–73, 75, 78, 86, 114, 119, 122

distant reading, 21–22, 127

distant writing, 21–23, 127, 129, 130, 136, 139, 144–146, 152

driftwood, 149

Edbauer, Jenny, 16; structures of feeling, 16, 114, 122

Ekman, Ulrik, 72

electricity, 10, 19, 22–23, 49, 50–51, 94, 96, 128–129, 141, 146, 152–153

electrode, 153, 157–158

empathy: emotional bonds, 113

energy, 9, 10–11, 14–15, 19, 21–23, 26, 51, 57, 95, 133, 142–143, 146, 148–149, 152–153

epideictic rhetoric, 16–19, 86, 102, 119, 150

ethology, 110, 118

ethos, 20–21, 25

event space, 47, 57, 61, 63, 106, 158

eversion, 5, 10–12, 14–16, 19, 21, 31, 47, 50, 55–57, 60, 67, 110–111, 120–122, 126, 158

everyware, 4, 37–38, 67, 73

exigence, 25, 68–69

experience, 3–5, 12, 14–16, 20–21, 24, 34–35, 37–38, 57, 63, 67, 71, 86–87, 93, 111, 114, 119, 120, 126, 132, 135, 138–139, 153, 155, 158, 162

experimental, 24, 28, 32, 36–38, 44, 72, 82, 105–106, 116, 123, 125, 145–146

expressivism, 69, 147

Fahnestock, Jean, 81–82

Index

feedback loop, 24–25, 57, 101, 106, 124

Ferguson, Missouri, 156

flow, 10–12, 19, 21–22, 32, 35, 49–51, 55, 57, 96, 119, 129, 133–134, 148–149

flower, 112

focus, 6, 8, 12, 23–24, 39, 47, 71, 79, 96, 98, 104, 109–110, 114, 127, 135–136, 139, 141, 148

fold, 5, 19, 31, 59

forensic: oratory, 17

FPS (Frames Per Second), 115

Fraser, John, 40

functions, 15, 110

games, 12, 41, 59, 83–85, 104

gestures, 24, 102, 106, 107–108, 111, 119, 138–139, 141, 145

g-force, 46, 52

Gibson, William, 5, 11

GitHub, 105

glass, 145, 152, 162

Goldsworthy, Andrew, 148–149

Goodnight Lamp, 13

Google Glass, 102

great outdoors, 78, 82, 86, 89, 93, 100, 150, 160

Greek, Ancient, 22, 60, 130–131, 135

GUI (Graphical User Interface), 111–112, 161

hardware, 8, 11, 27, 45, 63, 95, 135

Harris, Roy, 22, 25, 129, 130, 131–135, 145

Hayles, Katherine, 57, 151

Hemingway, Ernest, 19, 20, 31

homo ludens, 112–113

Huizinga, Johan, 112–113

hypertext, 8, 32, 34, 72, 123–124, 126

IDE (Integrated Development Environment), 29, 53

Igoe, Tom, 3, 11

image, 34, 56, 89, 106, 114, 120, 122, 125–126, 158

individuality, 110

information: dance of, 38, 68, 73, 78, 87, 89, 93; overload, 68–69, 71

information age, 73, 76, 113, 127

Ingold, Tim, 25, 129, 135–142, 144–145, 155

Ingold's theory, 14, 23, 25, 59, 70, 108, 127, 130, 132, 135, 146–147, 149

innovation, 5, 6, 9, 15, 19, 37, 102–103, 145, 151

input technologies, 9

interfaces, 4, 8, 25, 61, 68, 87, 89, 102–103, 111–112, 123, 155

internet, 71

Internet of Things (IoT), 4

interobjectivity, 79, 86

invention: choric, 142, 144–145, 151–154, 157–158; transductive, 11–16, 19, 21–23, 25–26, 30–31, 35–38, 42, 45, 47–48, 57, 60, 114, 123, 125, 128–129, 133–135, 141, 146, 155, 157–158

invention, 4, 14–15, 23–26, 31, 36–38, 40, 42, 45, 56, 123, 127, 152, 154

iridescent shells, 75, 160

Jack of All Trades, 41

Jackson, Shelley, 32, 34

Jakobson, Roman, 40

Jameson, Frederic, 73

Index

Jasinski, James, 15
JSON (JavaScript Object Notation), 96

Kant, Immanuel, 73–74
Kendon, Adam, 107–108
keyboard, 6, 9, 26, 161
Kinect, 24–25, 28–29, 102–106, 111–112, 114–117, 119–125
Kress, Gunther, 132–133
Kurdi, Alan, 60

Lady Ada, 105
Lanham, Richard E., 19–24, 31–32, 67, 69, 75–78, 86, 94, 141–145
LDR (Light-Dependent Resistor), 53
LED (Light-Emitting Diode), 10–11, 92–96, 98–100
Levi-Strauss, Claude, 23, 36, 38–42, 44
line-making, 22, 127, 129, 135, 158
logocentrism, 22, 72, 139, 145
loops: feedback, 57, 120
Los Reyes, August, 112–114

magic, 39, 40–42, 44
Massimo, Banzi, 36, 38
McCorkle, Ben, 103, 109
medium, 34, 38, 69, 72, 109, 144
Meillassoux, Quentin, 73–74, 78
melody, 31, 77, 136–137
MEMS (Micro-Electro-Mechanical Systems), 36, 46–48
metaphor, 40
microcomponents, 10, 31, 38, 161
microcontroller: Arduino, 6, 26–27, 30, 61, 94–95, 129, 151
microprocesses, 23, 38
Microsoft, 24, 28, 102–106, 111–112

microtechnologies, 6, 23, 24, 38, 71
mobile army, 37–38, 42
MOMA (Museum of Modern Art), 3
Moretti, Franco, 21–22, 127, 129
movement, 6, 9, 27, 34, 49, 52, 54–57, 60, 64, 66, 74, 101, 103–104, 106–107, 111, 118–120, 123–124, 126, 133–134, 139–140, 153, 156
music, 112, 135–139, 159
mythical thought, 41
myths, 41

nature, 39, 43–44, 83, 111, 140, 148–149
neolithic thought, 39, 44
networks, 5, 6, 13, 45, 64, 70–71, 80, 87, 94, 98, 140
Nietzsche, Frederic, 36–39, 75, 94
notation: history of, 136, 140
NUI (Natural User Interface), 4, 72, 102–103, 105–106, 111–112, 114, 145, 151–152, 158–159
numbers, 4, 10, 50, 51, 55, 64, 66, 68, 89, 94, 96, 98, 101, 110, 115–116, 122–123, 126–127, 133–134, 153, 160
object, 15, 48, 57, 79; attention, 76–77; everyware, 38, 67; interactive, 4, 47, 53–55, 93–94, 149, 153; ontography, 80–86; Twitter, 96–97
object-oriented philosophy, 24, 79, 81
Olbrechts-Tyteca, Lucie, 17–18
Ong, Walter, 109, 137–139
onto-allegorical, 67, 86–88, 99

Index

ontograph: of events, 17, 53–54, 59, 61, 63, 80, 82–83, 87, 90, 92, 96–98, 115, 122–124, 140

ontographic, dramatic, 35, 44–45, 68–69, 71–72, 83, 111

ontography, 24, 67, 75, 78, 80–81, 83

ontology, 84, 118, 160

opacity, 126, 152

open source, 103, 105

operations, 39, 41, 79–80, 83–84, 86, 116

orators, 17–18, 21, 107–108

parataxis, 31

Patchwork Girl, 32, 34

patterns, 6, 22, 88, 99–100, 124, 126–127, 132, 141–142, 153

PC Era, 68, 69–70

periphery, 8, 68–69, 71

persuasion, 14–16, 18–19, 75

phonetic thought, 22, 25, 127, 161

pins, 26, 94, 95, 155

PIR (Pyroelectric Passive Infrared) sensor, 9

post-dialectical, 73

power, 8, 37, 43, 45, 70, 81, 94–95, 109, 114, 125, 142, 160

processes, 5, 11–15, 19, 22–23, 30–31, 36, 38–42, 47, 54–57, 63, 65, 71, 80, 86, 94, 98, 120–121, 124–126, 128–129, 131, 135, 148

processing language, 29–30, 63, 88, 90, 98–100, 120, 125

prose, 19, 21, 31–32, 67, 69, 142, 144

quadrant, 98

Quintilian, Marcus Fabius, 106–107

radiance, 18, 86, 150

Rain Room, 3–5, 12, 14, 16, 19, 35, 78

rainfall, 35

Random International, 3, 78

rationalism, 113

representation, 19, 81, 86, 120, 131–132, 139

RGB (Red-Green-Blue), 105–106, 114

rhetoric, 14–18, 21, 23–25, 31, 37–38, 42, 45, 69, 73, 102–103, 106–112, 139, 141, 146–148, 150, 161; digital, 15, 23–24, 35, 46, 70, 72–73, 75, 78, 86, 114, 119, 122

rhythm, 19, 21, 31, 32, 64, 81, 135–136, 143

Ridolfo, Jim, 103, 109

Rosenfield, Lawrence W., 16–19, 86, 119, 150

Saper, Craig, 72, 93

Saussure, Ferdinand de, 131, 137, 139

science, 36, 38–45, 47

SDK (Software Development Kit), 28, 106

sensors, 9–10, 13, 19, 24–25, 28, 36, 47, 50–57, 63, 103–106, 114–116, 119–125, 128, 149, 151–153, 155, 159

Serial Monitor, 50, 53

skeuomorph, 151

slide potentiometer, 9

smartphone, 8, 70, 152

software, 8, 10–14, 22, 28, 44, 46, 50, 55–57, 63, 65, 67, 80, 87, 94, 100, 105, 120, 126, 128–129, 135, 154, 155

solder, 92, 94, 161

sound, 10, 61, 89, 100, 126, 133–134, 136–137, 139, 142–143, 151, 153, 157–158

space, 4, 8–9, 12, 25, 31, 49–50, 57, 61, 63, 72, 92, 104, 110V 111, 118, 120, 122–126, 130, 140, 142, 158, 162

SparkFun Electronics, 9, 11, 27, 36, 46

speech, 18, 22, 25, 31, 75, 107–108, 116, 127, 129, 130–139, 146, 149

Spinoza, Baruch, 110

Studdert-Kennedy, Michael, 133–134, 149

style, 19–21, 23–24, 31–32, 34–35, 37, 42, 45, 81, 86, 108, 142–144, 150, 155

suasion, 5, 12, 14–16, 19, 21, 31, 37–39, 42, 45, 47, 50, 54, 55–57, 63, 70, 110–111, 123, 145

subject, 57, 74, 79, 130, 147

surface, 10, 25, 37–38, 49, 52, 118, 137–141, 144–145, 148, 152–153

surreal, 4, 12

surround sound, 120, 126

swipe, 142, 144–145, 151–152

Tablet PC, 144–145, 151

threshold, 46, 51, 55, 64, 110, 158

tinkerer, 38–39, 41, 44

touchscreen, 9

transduction, 11–14, 16, 19, 21, 26, 31, 39, 47, 50, 52, 54–56, 63, 94, 98, 101, 111, 122, 126, 148, 154, 158, 161

transductive process, 11–13, 15, 22, 30, 47, 128–129

Twitter, 66, 67, 87–90, 92–93, 96, 98

ubiquitous computing, 4, 23–24, 67–68, 70–73, 86, 91

Ulmer, Gregory, 72, 142

uncountry, 161

users, 6, 9, 34, 36, 55, 70–71, 88, 92, 96–98, 102, 111–112, 114, 151–152, 156, 159–160, 162

vector, 110–111, 122, 134, 149

vertical-visual coordinate, 142–143

video, 3, 13, 26, 51, 87, 89, 92, 105, 144, 151

visualization, 26, 55–56, 64, 98, 120–126, 142, 143, 151, 157

Visualization Dashboard, 26, 55–56, 64, 65, 98, 123–126, 151, 157–158

Vitanza, Victor J., 59, 141, 146–148, 155

voice, 102, 104, 107–108, 111–112, 129, 137, 139, 159

voltage, 10, 13, 50–52, 153

Wainwright, Oliver, 3, 12

Warhol, Andy, 77–78

water, 4, 12, 35, 49, 55, 60–61, 63–64, 148–149, 152–153

wayve, 75, 92–93, 95, 97, 99, 141, 146–148

Waze app, 6, 7

Weiser, Mark, 23–24, 66, 68–75, 159

Welch, Kathleen, 109

Wood, Jeremy, 12

Woolf, Virginia, 142–144, 148

WordCram, 90, 98

Wordle, 99

writer: distant, 4, 8, 14, 21, 23, 25, 31–32, 67, 69, 72, 75, 127, 129, 130, 132–133, 135, 139, 142, 145, 146–150, 153, 154, 158, 161–162

Index

writing, 60, 67, 68, 69, 129; choric, 144–145; computers and writing, 8, 14; historical meaning, 131–133; line-making, 23, 25, 135, 139–141; pre-alphabetic, 25, 130; third wayve, 146-148; Weiser, 6, 72; and ontography, 86, 89; and speech, 134–140; with electricity, 22-23

Wysocki, Anne, 72

Xbox, 105
XEROX Parc, 23

Yancey, Kathleen Blake, 103
YouTube, 3, 87, 92

About the Author

David M Rieder is Associate Professor of English, faculty member of the Communication, Rhetoric, and Digital Media PhD program, and Co-Director of Circuit Research Studio at North Carolina State University. His research interests are at the intersections of digital media theory, digital rhetoric/writing, and digital humanities. Recent scholarly and creative works include the co-edited collection, *Small Tech*, essays and 'born digital' works in *Kairos, Computers and Composition Online, Hyperrhiz, Present Tense, Itineration*, and *Enculturation*. Rieder is a programmer and maker whose work includes digital media collaborations for public audiences. Recent examples of public collaborations include three works in Raleigh's Contemporary Art Museum (CAM).

Photograph of the author.

CPSIA information can be obtained
at www.ICGtesting.com
Printed in the USA
BVHW020649140119
537477BV00056B/425/P